By THE Rivers Of Babylon

In A Strange Land

Psalm 137 is one of the best known of the Biblical psalms.

Its opening lines, "By the rivers of Babylon..."

By

Huma Kirmani

In A Strange Land

By the rivers of Babylon, there we sat down

Ye-eah we wept, when we remembered Zion.

By the rivers of Babylon, there we sat down

Ye-eah we wept, when we remembered Zion.

When the wicked

Carried us away in captivity

Required from us a song

Now how shall we sing the lord's song in a strange land?

When the wicked

Carried us away in captivity

Requiring of us a song

Now how shall we sing the lord's song in a strange land?

Yeah, yeah, yeah, yeah, yeah let the words of our mouth

And the meditations of our heart

Be acceptable in thy sight here tonight

Let the words of our mouth and the meditation of our hearts

Be acceptable in thy sight here tonight

By the rivers of Babylon, there we sat down

Ye-eah we wept, when we remembered Zion.

By the rivers of Babylon, there we sat down

Ye-eah we wept, when we remembered Zion.

By the rivers of Babylon (dark tears of Babylon)

There we sat down (you got to sing a song)

Ye-eah we wept, (sing a song of love)

When we remember Zion. (yeah yeah yeah yeah yeah)

By the rivers of Babylon (rough bits of Babylon)

There we sat down (you hear the people cry)

Ye-eah we wept, (they need their god)

When we remember Zion. (Ooh, have the power)

"Rivers of Babylon" is a Rastafarian song written and recorded by Brent Dowe and Trevor McNaughton of the Jamaican reggae group The Melodians in 1970. The lyrics are adapted from the texts of Psalms 19 and 137 in the Hebrew Bible. The Melodeons' original version of the song appeared in the soundtrack album of the 1972 movie The Harder They Come, making it internationally known.

The song was popularized in Europe by the 1978 Boney M. cover version, which was awarded a platinum disc and is one of the top ten all-time best-selling singles in the UK

Songwriters: BRENT DOWE, FRANK FARIAN, GEORGE REYAM, TREVOR MC NAUGHTONK.

Beautiful Babylon: Jewel of the Ancient World

Ruled by Hammurabi, restored by Nebuchadrezzar, conquered by Cyrus—this city in the heart of Mesopotamia was both desired and despised, placing it at the center stage of the dawn of history. Babylon is a real bricks-and-mortar place at the center of the vibrant Mesopotamian culture that it dominated for so many centuries.

Mesopotamia—"the land between two rivers"—gave birth to many of the world's first great cities. The splendid city of Babylon, located between the waters of the Euphrates and the Tigris some 60 miles south of Baghdad, was one of them. Unlike the many towns that fell and disappeared, Babylon was resilient, rising from its own ashes time and again, even as new conquerors invaded and took over. The pleasure its occupiers enjoyed came at a price, however, since the highly desired Babylon would always be seen as a prize for the taking.

Babylon has resonated in Judeo-Christian culture for centuries. The books of the Old Testament recount the exile of the Jews to Babylon following the sack of Jerusalem, by whose waters they "sat down and wept." By the time of the New Testament, the city had become a potent symbol: the corrupt earthly twin city to the pure, heavenly New Jerusalem.

Outside the biblical tradition, Babylon intrigued Greek and Roman writers, who added to the rich store of legends that have come down to the present day. The Greek historian Herodotus wrote about Babylon in the fifth century B.C. A number of inconsistencies in his account have led many scholars to believe that he never traveled there and that his text may be closer to hearsay than historical fact. Popular tales of Babylon's fantastic structures, like the Tower of Babel and the Hanging Gardens, may also be products of legends and confusion. Yet to historians and archaeologists, Babylon is a real bricks-and-mortar place at the center of the vibrant Mesopotamian culture that it dominated for so many centuries.

Babylon enjoyed its heyday during the seventh and sixth centuries B.C., when it was believed to be the largest city in the world. A new dynasty founded by a tribe known as the Chaldeans had wrested control from the Assyrians in the early 600s B.C. The second ruler of the Chaldean line became notorious for both cruelty and opulence: Nebuchadrezzar II, the king who sacked Jerusalem and sent the captive Jews to the capital of his new and increasingly powerful regional empire.

The psalm is a hymn expressing the yearnings of the Jewish people in exile following the Babylonian conquest of Jerusalem in 607 BCE. The rivers of Babylon are the Euphrates river, its tributaries, and the Tigris river. In its whole form, the psalm reflects the yearning for Jerusalem as well as hatred for the Holy City's enemies with sometimes violent imagery. Rabbinical sources attributed the poem to the prophet Jeremiah,[1] and the Septuagint version of the psalm bears the superscription.

Babylon is the most famous city from ancient Mesopotamia whose ruins lie in modern-day Iraq 59 miles (94 kilometres) southwest of Baghdad. The name is thought to derive from bav-il or bav-ilim which, in the Akkadian language of the time, meant 'Gate of God' or `Gate of the Gods' and `Babylon' coming from Greek.

After being destroyed and then rebuilt by the Assyrians, Babylon became the capital of the Neo-Babylonian Empire from 609 to 539 BC. The Hanging Gardens of Babylon was one of the Seven Wonders of the Ancient World.

Babylon băb´əlŏn [key], ancient city of Mesopotamia. One of the most important cities of the ancient Middle East, it was on the Euphrates River and was north of the cities that flourished in S Mesopotamia in the 3d millennium BC It became important when Hammurabi made it the capital of his kingdom of Babylonia .

The Battle of Opis, fought in September 539 BC, was a major engagement between the armies of Persia under Cyrus the Great and the Neo-Babylonian Empire under Nabonidus during the Persian invasion of Mesopotamia. ... It resulted in a decisive victory for the Persians.It is certain that they spoke a Semitic language related to modern Arabic and Hebrew. In the second millennium, the Akkadian language was spoken and written all over Mesopotamia, although there was a southern (Babylonian) and a northern (Assyrian) variant.

Cyrus the Great (d. c.530 bc), king of Persia 559–530 bc and founder of the Achaemenid dynasty, father of Cambyses. He defeated the Median empire in 550 bc and went on to conquer Asia Minor, Babylonia, Syria, Palestine, and most of the Iranian plateau.The Neo-Babylonian Empire, also known as the Chaldean Empire, was a period.of Mesopotamian history which began in 626 BC and ended in 539 BC. During the preceding three centuries, Babylonia had been ruled by their fellow Akkadian speakers and northern neighbours, Assyria.

The exact dates of the Lydian conquest are unknown, but it must have taken place between Cyrus's overthrow of the Median kingdom (550 BC) and his conquest of Babylon.

In 550 B.C.E. Cyrus the Great, the leader of the Persians, conquered the Medes and united the Iranian people under one ruler for the first time. Cyrus became the first king of the Persian Empire and went on to establish one of the largest empires in world.

"Freedom of opinion and other basic rights"

The Shah described Cyrus as the first ruler in history to give his subjects "freedom of opinion and other basic rights". In 1968, the Shah opened the first United Nations Conference on Human Rights in Tehran by saying that the Cyrus Cylinder was the precursor to the modern Universal Declaration of Human Rights. Known today as the Cyrus Cylinder, this ancient record has now been recognized as the world's first charter of human rights. It is translated into all six official languages of the United Nations and its provisions parallel the first four Articles of the Universal Declaration of Human Rights.The Universal Declaration of Human Rights (UDHR) is a declaration adopted by the United Nations General Assembly on 10 December 1948 at the Palais de Chaillot in Paris, France. The Declaration arose directly from the experience of the two world wars.For critics, the Universal Declaration of Human Rights is a Western-biased document which fails to account for the cultural norms and values which exist in the rest of the world. More than that, it is an attempt to impose Western values on everybody else. In some ways they are right.Cyrus the Great is said in the Bible to have liberated the Jews from the Babylonian captivity to resettle and rebuild Jerusalem, earning him an honored.

What Is Babylon?

Babylon was once a great and feared kingdom. Today, its capital city is a heap of dried bricks and stones in Iraq. What does it represent in the future?

Babylon, past and future, is a significant theme in the Bible.

The Bible goes to great lengths to clearly tell us about two different (but similar), literal Babylons: ancient, historical Babylon and modern, prophesied Babylon the Great. The Bible tells us that, after the Great Flood, Noah's great-grandson Nimrod founded the world's first multi-national, multi-ethnic and multi-cultural empire

Babel (Hebrew), or Babylon (Greek), was one of the cities of an ancient kingdom established by Nimrod early in mankind's history (Genesis 10:10). It is considered by some to be the place where life began and was the site where humans attempted to build a tower that would extend up to heaven (Genesis 11:1-4).Seeing what humans were trying to do, God confused their language so they could not complete the tower they had begun. "Babel" means confusion and was a fitting name for this city whose residents were not obeying God. This same city became the epitome of all idolatrous worship and the capital city of an empire with its name.Some 1,500 years after its founding, God spoke of Babylon through the prophet Isaiah, "Babylon is fallen, is fallen! And all the carved images of her gods He has broken to the ground" (Isaiah 21:9).

The kingdom of Babylon would continue for another 200 years beyond the life of Isaiah until 539 B.C. The city would continue to be inhabited up until the Islamic invasions around A.D. 650.The prophecy of Isaiah had a dual meaning. It not only referred to ancient Babylon, but also to a second Babylon, the Babylon of the book of Revelation (Revelation 14:8; Revelation 18:2).

The Bible records that King Nebuchadnezzar had a very troubling dream in his second year (around 603 B.C.), not long after the first Jewish captives came to Babylon. God gave the interpretation of the dream to a young Jewish captive and prophet named Daniel who, in turn, explained it to the king. Daniel told King Nebuchadnezzar, "You, O king, are a king of kings. For the God of heaven has given you a kingdom, power, strength, and glory; … you are this head of gold [seen in the dream]" (Daniel 2:37-38).

As a result of the interpretation, Daniel was highly respected and had considerable influence with King Nebuchadnezzar. Three times the king would recognize the God of Daniel as God (Daniel 2:47; 3:29; 4:34).

It was King Nebuchadnezzar II who built the magnificent hanging gardens, the incredible double walls 15 miles square around the city, the beautiful Ishtar Gate, and the many monuments of splendor that marked the zenith of Babylon's history. The fall of the Babylonian Empire came more than 20 years after his death, but its fall was prophesied more than two centuries before his birth.

Modern, Prophesied Babylon the Great

Of course, modern, prophesied Babylon is not named in the Bible because she was not in existence when the Bible was written. When confronted with plain evidence from history, current events, and the Bible, the identity of modern Babylon is crystal clear, undeniable, and irrefutable.

Then, why do very few Americans acknowledge that Babylon is the United States of America? This commentator has often asked himself that question. Citizens of other nations do not seem so blinded to that reality. I think it is because it is just very, very difficult for us to be objective about something in which we have a very high personal stake; especially if our whole lives we have been taught something different. Also, at the present time modern Babylon the Great is disguised as a "Christian" nation.

Modern Babylon must be very similar to ancient Babylon. Think about all the characteristics of ancient Babylon listed above: totalitarian, dictatorial government led by a self-deified ruler; eclectic, idolatrous religion blended with the government; strong sense of national pride and patriotism; luxury and wealth - dominates world economy and trade; by far the most powerful military in the world; powerful defense - seemingly "invincible"; world cultural center; center for world government; the "melting pot" of the world; a very immoral nation, tolerating all kinds of sexual immorality and perversion; a "party" nation, centered on entertainment and revelry; imperialistic - dominating the governments of other nations of the world.

President George W. Bush garnered more powers for the top executive than any other President in history. While he was in college, President Bush (as did his father, George H.W. Bush) became a member of Skull and Bones - an organization based on the belief that its members have been "born again" into a state of superhuman spirituality (their own spirit, not the Spirit of the Lord Yahuah). And President Barack Obama, with widespread and intrusive enforcement of the Patriot Act, continued that trend during his term. In the event of another "national emergency" like that of 9-11-2001, an economic crisis, or World War III, the President could declare national martial law overnight, just as Adolf Hitler did in Germany on November 9, 1938, the date he started having Jews and others who opposed his government killed and thousands of them shipped off to concentration camps. Obama also practices self-worship, believing that the way one rises above the common and mundane is to develop the god-person within. President Obama also, by supporting the Muslim Brotherhood and opening America's borders to millions of illegal immigrants and Islamic refugees, set the stage for the prophesied takeover of the U.S. by Middle Eastern terrorists. Plus, in her final form, just before her total destruction "by fire," modern Babylon will be ruled by a totalitarian government with a mandated religion (Islam?), exactly like ancient Babylon.

One might object to the suggestion that America is imperialistic. It would probably boggle your mind to know how many nations of the world, including Honduras, Uruguay, Afghanistan, Iraq, several African nations, and many others around the world are just client states of the USA; their economies would immediately collapse if America's multi-national corporations pulled out or stopped importing their goods. Therefore, the USA calls the shots in how those countries are run: Their "elected" leaders are virtual puppet governors controlled by the USA. And now, also exactly as prophesied (note the amazing simililarity between the USA and Babylon the Great of Revelation 18), the current US president Donald Trump, with his grandiose pledge to "make America greater than ever before," and loading his administration with powerful business and military leaders, conservative judges and Republican Congress members, shows indications of indeed making America the most powerful economic, political and military nation/empire in history.

But, the greatest similarity of all between ancient and modern Babylon is religion. Now many, especially American Christians, will flatly deny that assertion.

Virtually all Americans have been taught all of our lives and believe that the United States of America is basically a Christian nation - founded on Christian principles by Christians. In fact, we have been taught, especially in the churches, that America is "God's" Redeemer Nation, and the whole world will be brought to Yahushua ("Jesus") the Messiah ("Christ") through the USA, right;nothing could be farther from the truth. George Washington, Thomas Jefferson, Benjamin Franklin and most of the other Founding Fathers of America claimed to be Christians, but were really Deists, or a combination of Deist and humanist who incorporated Christian principles into their belief system. Therefore, we will call them "Christian Deists." You may ask, "What is a Christian Deist, and what is the difference between a Christian Deist and a true Believer in Yahushua the Messiah?" As you will see, the difference is satanically subtle, but real. Webster defines "Deism" as "natural religion" - believing in the Creator, but not in miracles or the intervention of that god in human affairs. In other words, a "Deist" is someone who believes in one "God" who created the heavens and the earth and everything that is in them, and that He created human beings in His own image - put His good, spiritual nature in us. So far, so good, according to the Bible. But then, according to the Deists, "God" left the world pretty much to run on its own, and he left man, who had "God's" spiritual goodness, wisdom, and power within, in charge - to manage and take care of the world. But man blew it; he let sin and corruption into the world. Man lost control. And it has been downhill since that time. But, according to the Deists, man still has "God's" nature; he is still basically good and has the knowledge, wisdom and power, somewhere in his being, to regain dominion of the world. We just needed a god-man, a perfect, sinless man, a messiah and savior, to show us the way back to our godlikeness. And, to Christians, that Messiah and Savior is "Jesus Christ." So, all that Christians need to do is to believe in Yahushua, follow his teachings, and by the wisdom and power of Yahuah's Spirit, which He put in them in The Beginning, come back into touch with their basic, natural goodness, bring the rest of the citizens of the world into actualization of their basic God-likeness, and reestablish Paradise on Earth and their dominion over it.

Bringing Babylon back from the dead

Babylon was one of the glories of the ancient world, its walls and mythic hanging gardens listed among the Seven Wonders.

Founded about 4,000 years ago, the ancient city was the capital of 10 dynasties in Mesopotamia, considered one of the earliest cradles of civilization and the birthplace of writing and literature.

But following years of plunder, neglect and conflict, the Babylon of today scarcely conjures that illustrious history.

In recent years, the Iraqi authorities have reopened Babylon to tourists, hoping that one day the site will draw visitors from all over the globe. But despite the site's remarkable archaeological value and impressive views, it is drawing only a smattering of tourists, drawn by a curious mix of ancient and more recent history.

THE GULF WAR & PROPHECY

The Gulf War is on everyone's mind and in many prayers. Its ultimate outcome has never been in doubt. Prolongation of the destruction and bloodshed is due solely to the gigantic ego and evil of Saddam Hussein, the Arab Hitler, who is needlessly destroying both his army and country just as der Fuehrer did.

There will be an ultimate requirement to establish an unprecedented Middle East peace under a new world order. One of the benefits may well be a weakening, if not crumbling, of the Islamic Curtain, which, like the shattering of the Iron Curtain, should bring disillusionment with Islam and a new openness to Christianity in Islamic lands. The restoration of the Kuwaiti government should see major steps in the direction of democracy and the freedoms conducive to human rights and the proclamation of the gospel—changes that hopefully will spill over into Saudi Arabia and other neighboring countries. Fanaticism, however, will also reign.

Many asked, if at all, this conflict fits into Bible prophecy and what role it will play in preparing the world for the Antichrist. Some Christian leaders are suggesting that because Saddam had been rebuilding ancient Babylon, Iraq is therefore the Babylon of the last days mentioned in Revelation 17 and 18and that the destruction now underway fulfills last-days prophecies. On neither the contrary, neither Iraq nor ancient

Babylon (which has been in ruins for 2,200 years) nor Saddam's rebuilt Babylon (if he succeeds, which is doubtful) fits the detailed description of MYSTERY, BABYLON in Revelation.

Saddam Hussein has portrayed himself as the new Nebuchadnezzar who would, like Nebuchadnezzar of old, destroy Israel. In taking such a role he sealed his doom ("I will...curse him that curseth thee" - Gen:12:3). Saddam survived the war he should be tried and condemned as a war criminal. His crimes were many and horrendous, having brought death to more than 1 million people and the torture, rape and plunder to countless more. It is being said that even in defeat he emerged as the great hero of the Arab world. That may be so in the eyes of some fanatical Muslims, but thinking Arabs saw him as the embodiment of evil. It seemed likely that his project to rebuild Babylon—a luxury unaffordable to a devastated Iraq—will be abandoned.

Saddam Hussein has portrayed himself as the new Nebuchadnezzar who would, like Nebuchadnezzar of old, destroy Israel. In taking such a role he sealed his doom ("I will...curse him that curseth thee" - Gen:12:3). If Saddam survived the war he should be tried and condemned as a war criminal. His crimes are many and horrendous, having brought death to more than 1 million people and the torture, rape and plunder to countless more. It is being said that even in defeat he will emerge as the great hero of the Arab world. That may be so in the eyes of some fanatical Muslims, but thinking Arabs will see him as the embodiment of evil. It seems likely that his project to rebuild Babylon—a luxury unaffordable to a devastated Iraq—will be abandoned.

There were predictions that Israel would be drawn into the Gulf War (as Saddam has attempted to do), thus shattering the coalition and causing Arab nations to unite on the side of Iraq. The result was allegedly be the destruction of the United States both militarily and economically. On the contrary, Iraq's ability to bully her neighbors was destroyed and a new climate for peace created in the region.

Where does the Gulf War fit into prophecy? It is not specifically mentioned. The real significance of this war in the scheme of biblical prophecy is found in the repeated statements by President Bush, Soviet and other world leaders that Saddam Hussein's takeover of Kuwait was a threat to the new world order. The Gulf War was not being fought primarily to lower the price of gas nor even to liberate Kuwait, but to defined, established and preserved a new world order that will, unwittingly, set the stage for Antichrist.

Babylon in the Gulf War

The city just 85km (52 miles) south of Baghdad, about a two hour drive, dependent on checkpoints still bears the marks of ham-fisted attempts at restoration by former Iraqi dictator Saddam Hussein, and a subsequent occupation by U.S. forces in 2003. "They occupied Babylon. They wouldn't let anyone in," says Hussein Saheb, a guard at the historical sites at Babylon, recalling the day U.S. tanks rolled into view, before forces set up camp.

When U.S. forces arrived in 2003, they occupied the palace, which lies adjacent to Nebuchadnezzar's palace and overlooks the Euphrates River, and left their own mark. Today, a basketball hoop remains in Babylon, while concertina wire left behind by the military is used to prevent visitors from climbing over a 2,500-year-old lion statue -- an ancient symbol of the city. Troops from the US-led force in Iraq have caused widespread damage and severe contamination to the remains of the ancient city of Babylon, according to a damning report released today by the British Museum. Babylon, a city renowned for its beauty and its splendour 1,000 years before Europe built anything comparable, was chosen as the site for a US military base in April 2003, just after the invasion of Iraq.

Military commanders set up their camp in the heart of one of the world's most important archaeological sites and surrounded the enclosed part of the ancient city. At least 2,000 troops were installed, daily passing iconic relics like the enormous basalt Lion of Babylon sculpture.

In September 2003 the base was passed to a Polish-led force, which held it until today's formal handover of the site to the Iraqi culture ministry. The American record elsewhere in Iraq is no better. At Babylon, American and Polish forces built a military depot, despite objections from archaeologists. John Curtis, the British Museum's authority on Iraq's many archaeological sites, reported on a visit in December 2004 that he saw "cracks and gaps where somebody had tried to gouge out the decorated bricks forming the famous dragons of the Ishtar Gate" and a "2,600-year-old brick pavement crushed by military vehicles".

Other observers say that the dust stirred up by US helicopters has sandblasted the fragile brick facade of the palace of Nebuchadnezzar II, king of Babylon from 605 to 562 BC. Between May and August 2004, the wall of the Temple of Nabu and the roof of the Temple of Ninmah, both of the sixth century BC, collapsed as a result of the movement of helicopters. Nearby, heavy machines and vehicles stand parked on the remains of a Greek theater from the era of Alexander of Macedon [Alexander the Great].

And none of this even begins to deal with the massive, ongoing looting of historical sites across Iraq by freelance grave and antiquities robbers, preparing to stock the living rooms of Western collectors. The unceasing chaos and lack of security brought to Iraq in the wake of our invasion have meant that a future peaceful Iraq may hardly have a patrimony to display. It is no small accomplishment of the Bush administration to have plunged the cradle of the human past into the same sort of chaos and lack of security as the Iraqi present. If amnesia is bliss, then the fate of Iraq's antiquities represents a kind of modern paradise.

In the months before he ordered the invasion of Iraq, President George W Bush and his senior officials spoke of preserving Iraq's "patrimony" for the Iraqi people. At a time when talking about Iraqi oil was taboo, what he meant by patrimony was exactly that – Iraqi oil. In their "joint statement on Iraq's future" of April 8, 2003, Bush and British Prime Minister Tony Blair declared, "We reaffirm our commitment to protect Iraq's natural resources, as the patrimony of the people of Iraq, which should be used only for their benefit." In this they were true to their word. Among the few places American soldiers actually did guard during and in the wake of their invasion were oil fields and the Oil Ministry in Baghdad. But the real Iraqi patrimony, that invaluable human inheritance of thousands of years, was another matter. At a time when American pundits were warning of a future "clash of civilizations", our occupation forces were letting perhaps the greatest of all human patrimonies be looted and smashed.

Bush's supporters have talked endlessly about his global "war on terrorism" as a "clash of civilizations". But the civilization in the process of destroying in Iraq is part of heritage. It is also part of the world's patrimony. Before invasion of Afghanistan, US condemned the Taliban for dynamiting the monumental third century AD Buddhist statues at Bamiyan in March, 2001. Those were two gigantic statues of remarkable historical value and the barbarism involved in their destruction blazed in headlines and horrified commentaries in our country. Today, US government is guilty of far greater crimes when it comes to the destruction of a whole universe of antiquity, and few here, when they consider Iraqi attitudes toward the American occupation, even take that into consideration. But what we do not care to remember, others may recall all too well.

A New World Order

Gorbachev was the first world leader in modern times to invoke the image of a new world order. In his historic address to the UN on December 7, 1988, he declared,

"Further global progress is now possible only through a quest for universal consensus in the movement towards a new world order."

The Pope had taken up the refrain and so other world leaders in many countries. Indeed, the world now seems almost unanimous in its acceptance of such a goal. Sadly, such high hopes are a delusion!

George Bush claimed to be a born-again Christian. As President, he was working diligently to establish world peace. Is that not a worthy goal? And are not all Christians to pray for peace?

In a speech January 16, 1991, Billy Graham declared,

"There come times when we have to fight for peace."

He went on to say that out of the present war in the Gulf may "come a new peace and, as suggested by the President, a new world order. What should the Christian's attitude be toward the hoped-for new world order?

The Bible foretells the establishment of two new world orders in the last days:

 The first to be ruled by Antichrist and the second by Christ himself. We seem to be very close to that first event, and thus to the Rapture which must precede it. Considering the surprising transition by which Eastern Bloc countries are becoming part of a United States of Europe (depending upon what happens to Gorbachev and the Soviet Union), it seemed likely that the resolution of the Gulf War will be another giant step toward global peace and the revival of the Roman Empire over which Antichrist will reign.

One thing is clear: the new order on the agenda of both secular and religious leaders could not possibly be the millennial kingdom over which Christ will reign, but its counterfeit which would be ruled by Antichrist). A "peaceable life," however, is not the same as global peace under a new world order established by mankind in disobedience to God. Scripture warns that "the way of peace have they not known" (Rom:3:17) The Bible presents the only basis for world peace. It must be in concert with righteousness: "righteousness and peace have kissed each other" (Ps:85:10); "the kingdom of God is...righteousness and peace, and joy in the Holy Ghost" (Rom:14:17); "there is no peace...unto the wicked" (Isa:48:22

; 57:21). True worldwide peace can only be established by "the God of peace" (Rom:15:33;16:20; 1 Thes:5:23

; Heb:13:20, etc.) through the "gospel of peace" (Rom:10:15). In no other way can sinful mankind be reconciled to God—and without that reconciliation there can be no genuine peace.

Yes, a forgotten purpose of the gospel is to bring worldwide peace. The early disciples "preach[ed] peace by Jesus Christ: (He is Lord of all)." (Acts:10:36). The angels announced that good news at the birth of Christ: "Glory to God in the highest, and on earth peace, good will toward men" (Lk 2:14). Peace on earth comes only through God being glorified and obeyed and His Christ reigning supreme. Thus, a major purpose of Christ's death for our sins was to make "peace through the blood of his cross" (Col:1:20). In preaching the gospel, the early Christians declared the good news of "peace with God through our Lord Jesus Christ" (Rom:5:1).

The real test is whether we truly long to make that exchange now when life is vibrant, exciting and full of health and promise—or only when we face death and are forced by illness or old age to leave this evil world. Of course, everyone wants to exchange sickness, death and hell for heaven—but do we want to make that exchange, or do we have other plans and ambitions that mean more to us than being with Him?

The looming war in Iraq is likely to take a heavy toll in terms of lives and property. But in a country regarded as the "Cradle of Civilization," there may also be substantial harm to irreplaceable cultural heritage in the form of damage to ancient structures, archaeological sites, and artifacts.

Iraq is the land of ancient Mesopotamia, where peoples in the fertile ground between the Tigris and Euphrates rivers domesticated animals, began agriculture, and gave rise to the earliest cities some 6,000 years ago.

But Iraq's rich heritage, a source of enduring pride to humanity, has been under stress since the Gulf War of the early 1990s. A new outbreak of hostilities may put archaeological sites, historic architecture, and priceless artifacts in further jeopardy, archaeologists fear.

In Iraq, sites of tremendous scientific and historic importance are part and parcel of the landscape.

The first immediate danger to Iraq's cultural sites is bombing or combat damage. In the first Gulf War, damage of this kind appeared to have been fairly limited. Shellfire damaged the brickwork of the ziggurat at Ur, which was constructed in 2100 B.C. In Mosul, a 10th century church was partially destroyed by bombing in 1990. Cracks appeared in other ancient sites as the concussion of nearby explosions rocked ancient foundations.

PERSIAN GULF WAR

Iraqi leader Saddam Hussein ordered the invasion and occupation of neighboring Kuwait in early August 1990. Alarmed by these actions, fellow Arab powers such as Saudi Arabia and Egypt called on the United States and other Western nations to intervene. Hussein defied United Nations Security Council demands to withdraw from Kuwait by mid-January 1991, and the Persian Gulf War began with a massive U.S.-led air offensive known as Operation Desert Storm. After 42 days of relentless attacks by the allied coalition in the air and on the ground, U.S. President George H.W. Bush declared a cease-fire on February 28; by that time, most Iraqi forces in Kuwait had either surrendered or fled. Though the Persian Gulf War was initially considered an unqualified success for the international coalition, simmering conflict in the troubled region led to a second Gulf War–known as the Iraq War.

On November 29, 1990, the U.N. Security Council authorized the use of "all necessary means" of force against Iraq if it did not withdraw from Kuwait by the following January 15. By January, the coalition forces prepared to face off against Iraq numbered some 750,000, including 540,000 U.S. personnel and smaller forces from Britain, France, Germany, the Soviet Union, Japan, Egypt and Saudi Arabia, among other nations. Iraq, for its part, had the support of Jordan (another vulnerable neighbor), Algeria, the Sudan, Yemen, Tunisia and the Palestinian Liberation Organization (PLO).

Early on the morning of January 17, 1991, a massive U.S.-led air offensive hit Iraq's air defenses, moving swiftly on to its communications networks, weapons plants, oil refineries and more. The coalition effort, known as Operation Desert Storm, benefited from the latest military technology, including Stealth bombers, Cruise missiles, so-called "Smart" bombs with laser-guidance systems and infrared night-bombing equipment. The Iraqi air force was either destroyed early on or opted out of combat under the relentless attack, the objective of which was to win the war in the air and minimize combat on the ground as much as possible.

Aftermath of the Persian Gulf War

Though the Gulf War was recognized as a decisive victory for the coalition, Kuwait and Iraq suffered enormous damage, and Saddam Hussein was not forced from power. Intended by coalition leaders to be a "limited" war fought at minimum cost, it would have lingering effects for years to come, both in the Persian Gulf region and around the world. In the immediate aftermath of the war, Hussein's forces brutally suppressed uprisings by Kurds in the north of Iraq and Shi'ites in the south. The United States-led coalition failed to support the uprisings, afraid that the Iraqi state would be dissolved if they succeeded. In the years that followed, U.S. and British aircraft continued to patrol skies and mandate a no-fly zone over Iraq, while Iraqi authorities made every effort to frustrate the carrying out of the peace terms, especially United Nations weapons inspections. This resulted in a brief resumption of hostilities in 1998, after which Iraq steadfastly refused to admit weapons inspectors. In addition, Iraqi force regularly exchanged fire with U.S. and British aircraft over the no-fly zone.

In 2002, the United States (now led by President George W. Bush, son of the former president) sponsored a new U.N. resolution calling for the return of weapons inspectors to Iraq; U.N. inspectors reentered Iraq that November. Amid differences between Security Council member states over how well Iraq had complied with those inspections, the United States and Britain began amassing forces on Iraq's border. Bush (without further U.N. approval) issued an ultimatum on March 17, 2003, demanding that Saddam Hussein step down from power and leave Iraq within 48 hours, under threat of war. Hussein refused, and the second Persian Gulf War—more generally known as the Iraq War—began three days later.

Kuwait wasn't a democracy before Saddam Hussein's army marched in, in 1990, and Kuwait isn't really a democracy today. No doubt it's a nicer place to live than Iraq, either during the Saddam era or during the subsequent American protectorate. But then, immiserating the Iraqi people—making it hard for ordinary citizens to get food, energy, health care, and other staples of life—was a purposeful part of the American strategy. And that part worked. So did the part about getting rid of Saddam Hussein—the main goal of George the Younger's prosecution of the war.

The other goal, which had democracy spreading from Iraq to Saudi Arabia to Syria and beyond, never came close to being realized. Egypt bounced longtime ruler Hosni Mubarak and gave democracy a brief whirl around the dance floor but didn't care for the result, which was soon discarded in favor of more military rule. The Arab Middle East today offers various forms of government. There is "royalty" of dubious provenance, as in Saudi Arabia and Kuwait—generally pro-American but ungrateful and untrustworthy. There are strongmen, but they can be longevity-challenged. Some regimes last weeks, others last decades, and none is a totally reliable ally. Then there is government by no government: the chaos of anarchy punctuated by atrocities in places like Syria, Libya, and much of Iraq. What you don't find, a quarter-century after this experiment began, are many robust democracies in the region (except for the ones that were already there—Israel and Turkey). The violent groups, needless to say, don't care much for the United States and, in fact, have spent years quarreling over whether the proper target for terrorist acts is the Great Satan far away or the Little Satans closer by.

Iraq: 10 Years after Gulf War

Ten years after the Gulf War, U.S. policy toward Iraq continues to suffer from an overreliance on military solutions, an abuse of the United Nations and international law, and a disregard for the human suffering resulting from sanctions.

Ten years after the Gulf War, U.S. policy toward Iraq continues to suffer from an overreliance on military solutions, an abuse of the United Nations and international law, and a disregard for the human suffering resulting from sanctions. Furthermore, Washington's actions have failed to dislodge Iraqi dictator Saddam Hussein from power.

The U.S. quietly supported Saddam Hussein during the 1980s through direct economic aid, indirect military aid, and the transfer of technologies with military applications. Washington rejected calls for sanctions when Iraq invaded Iran in 1980 and when it used chemical weapons against Iranian soldiers and Kurdish civilians. The U.S. Navy intervened in the Persian Gulf against Iran in 1987, further bolstering the Iraqi war effort. The Reagan and Bush administrations dismissed concerns about human rights abuses by Saddam's totalitarian regime. Such special treatment likely led the Iraqi dictator to believe that appeasement would continue.

Saddam Hussein's government had brought an impressive degree of prosperity to the Iraqi people, ranking them near the top of third world countries in terms of nutrition, education, health care, housing, and other basic needs. Yet he ruled with a brutality and a cult of personality that ranked his regime among the most totalitarian in the world.

Following a dispute with the government of Kuwait regarding debt repayment and oil policy during the summer of 1990, Iraq invaded the sheikdom in early August, soon annexing the country as its nineteenth province. The UN Security Council condemned the takeover and demanded Iraq's immediate withdrawal. Iraqi failure to comply led to comprehensive military and economic sanctions. Arab mediation efforts were short-circuited when the U.S. announced it was sending troops to Saudi Arabia to protect the kingdom via Operation Desert Shield, supported by forces from a couple of dozen other UN members. It soon became apparent that the U.S. was preparing for an offensive military action to dislodge Iraqi occupation forces, rejecting any negotiated settlement.

The Bush administration eventually won approval by the U.S. Congress and the UN Security Council to authorize the use of force; in the latter case, extraordinary pressure, including bribes and threats against other members were necessary to eke out a majority. The United States, with support from some allied governments, commenced a heavy bombing campaign in January 1991, inflicting severe damage on not only Iraqi military forces but much of the country's civilian infrastructure as well. The war, known as Operation Desert Storm, ended six weeks later, after a ground offensive in March liberated Kuwait from Iraqi control with minimal allied casualties but over 100,000 Iraqi deaths.

The cease-fire agreement imposed on Iraq by the U.S. in the name of the UN Security Council included unprecedented infringements on Iraq's sovereignty, particularly regarding the dismantling of weapons of mass destruction and related facilities, enforced through rigorous inspections by international monitors under the UN Special Commission on Iraq (UNSCOM). In addition, severe repression by Saddam's regime against rebellious Shiites in the south and Kurds in the north provided a pretext for the United States and its allies to create so-called "no-fly zones," restricting Iraq's military movements within its own borders.

Alleging that Iraq has not fully complied with provisions of the cease-fire agreement, particularly regarding cooperation with UNSCOM inspectors, the U.S. has successfully prevented the UN from lifting its sanctions more than ten years after they were first imposed. The result has been a humanitarian catastrophe, with hundreds of thousands of Iraqi civilians—primarily children—dying from malnutrition and preventable diseases resulting from the inability of Iraqis to get adequate food and medicine or the materials necessary to rebuild the war-damaged civilian infrastructure.

In April 1993 and September 1996, the U.S. engaged in a series of sustained air strikes against Iraq as punitive measures against alleged Iraqi transgressions. UNSCOM inspections were restricted by Iraq in December 1998, in part due to the use of the inspectors for espionage purposes by the U.S., prompting their withdrawal and a heavy four-day U.S. bombing campaign. Since early 1999, the U.S.—with the support of Great Britain—has engaged in unauthorized air strikes on an almost weekly basis.

The U.S. maintains a large-scale military presence in the region to this day. American aircraft patrol Iraqi air space and the U.S. Navy regularly inspects shipping to enforce both the sanctions and the restrictions on Iraqi military movements. U.S. policy has been defended as an effort to effectively restrict any potential Iraqi aggression against its neighbors, and as a means of creating internal political discontent. Critics charge that there are serious legal and ethical questions regarding U.S. policy and that it is actually strengthening the Iraqi dictator's hold on power.

Iraq still has not recovered from the 1991 war, during which it was on the receiving end of the heaviest bombing in world history. The U.S. has insisted on maintaining strict sanctions against Iraq to force compliance with demands to dismantle any capability of producing weapons of mass destruction and to address other outstanding issues from the cease-fire agreement. It is largely U.S. opposition that has prevented the UN from lifting the sanctions.

The sanctions have brought great hardships on the Iraqi people, as food prices are now 12,000 times what they were in 1990. It is Iraq's poor, particularly the children, who have suffered the most. Estimates of the total number of Iraqi deaths from malnutrition and preventable diseases as a result of the sanctions have ranged from a quarter million to over one million, the majority being children. UNICEF estimates that at least 4,500 Iraqi children are dying every month as a result of the sanctions. Indeed, perhaps there has been no other occasion during peacetime when so many people have been condemned to starvation and death from preventable diseases due to political decisions made overseas. The unseen impact of these sanctions on the social fabric of Iraq is perhaps even more severe.

The U.S. claims that such sanctions will lead to the downfall of Saddam Hussein's regime. However, Washington's policy against Iraq has had the ironic effect of strengthening Saddam's rule. Since the Iraqi people are now more dependent than ever on the government for their survival, they are even less likely to risk open defiance. U.S. policies simply have not harmed Iraq's ruling elites or weakened its repressive internal apparatus. Unlike the reaction to sanctions imposed prior to the war, Iraqi popular resentment lays the blame for the protracted suffering squarely on the United States, not on the totalitarian regime, whose ill-fated conquest of Kuwait prompted the events that led to the economic collapse of this once-prosperous country. In addition, Iraq's middle class, which would have most likely formed the political force capable of overthrowing Saddam's regime, has been reduced to penury; many have emigrated. It is not surprising that virtually all of Iraq's opposition movements oppose the U.S. policy of ongoing punitive sanctions and refuse to endorse the air strikes. Even after Saddam leaves, U.S. policies are creating a whole generation of Iraqis who will be stridently anti-American. Meanwhile, more and more countries are violating aspects of the sanctions regime, further undermining U.S. credibility.

U.S. officials have stated that sanctions would remain even if Iraq complied with United Nations inspectors, indicating a lack of genuine U.S. support for UN resolutions and giving the Iraqi regime virtually no incentive to comply. Moreover, the failure of both the United States and the United Nations to explicitly spell out what was needed in order for sanctions to be lifted contributed to Iraq's decision to suspend its cooperation with UN inspectors in December 1998.

Although Iraq's nuclear and chemical weapons capability has been successfully dismantled, there are still concerns about Iraq's biological weapons potential, though the U.S. has failed to make a credible case as to how Iraq could successfully deliver such weapons or what might motivate the regime to use them. And there is little evidence to suggest that U.S. air strikes have eliminated or reduced the country's biological weapons capability, which would be based upon small-scale operations that are difficult to find and eliminate through such military action.

The use of U.S. air strikes against Iraq subsequent to the weapons inspectors' departure has garnered very little support from the international community, including Iraq's neighbors, who would presumably be most threatened by an Iraqi biological weapons capability. The U.S. has been unable to make a credible case to clarify whom its policies are defending. The United States itself is certainly safe from Iraqi attacks, and most of Iraq's neighbors have strong armed forces of their own that are more than adequate to deter Iraq's severely crippled military.

In light of Washington's tolerance—and even quiet support—of Iraq's powerful military machine in the 1980s, the exaggerated claims in recent years of an imminent Iraqi military threat, after Iraq's military infrastructure was largely destroyed in the Gulf War, simply lack credibility. Indeed, the U.S. provided the seed stock for the very biological weapons that Washington claims the Iraqis may be developing. Though experts disagree about Iraq's ongoing potential for aggression, few actually believe current U.S. policy is making the region safer.

Only the UN Security Council has the prerogative to authorize military responses to violations of its resolutions; no single member state can do so unilaterally without explicit authorization. Were that the case, for example, Russia could bomb Israel for that government's ongoing violations of UN Security Council resolutions. The U.S. bombing campaigns, therefore, are illegal. In addition, the no-fly zones and other restrictions against Iraq's military activity within its borders were unilaterally imposed by the United States and Great Britain and are not based on any credible legal covenant.

U.S. policy toward Iraq seems to be a kind of foreign policy by catharsis, where air strikes and other punitive actions are imposed as "feel good" measures against an obstinate dictator. This may at times be politically popular, but it has little strategic value. Saddam Hussein and his inner circle remain safe in their bunkers as the bombs fall; civilians and unwilling conscripts continue to be the primary casualties.

Finally, U.S. double standards have greatly harmed American credibility in the region. Most Arabs and many other people around the world question why Washington insists that it is considered acceptable for Israel to have weapons of mass destruction and for the U.S. to bring weapons of mass destruction into the Middle East. This is particularly true since UN Security Council Resolution 687, which the U.S. claims to be enforcing through the sanctions and bombing, calls for "establishing in the Middle East a zone free from weapons of mass destruction and all missiles for their delivery."

The ongoing U.S. air strikes against Iraq are illegal and counterproductive and must end. Washington should continue to support an arms embargo on Iraq, but the U.S. should join the growing number of countries in the Middle East and around the world calling for a lifting of the economic sanctions that have brought so much suffering to Iraqi civilians.

The first step should be a U.S. promise to lift the economic sanctions once the UN secretary-general recognizes that Baghdad is in effective compliance with Security Council resolutions. Indeed, for sanctions to work, one needs a carrot as well as a stick, something Washington has failed to recognize. The United States, in consultation with other members of the Security Council, needs to clarify the positive responses that Iraq can expect in return for specific improvements in its behavior.

In addition, Washington must pledge to enforce other outstanding UN Security Council resolutions and not simply single out Iraq. As long as the United States allows allied regimes like Turkey, Morocco, and Israel to flaunt UN Security Council resolutions, any sanctimonious calls for strict compliance by the Iraqi government will simply be dismissed as hypocritical and mean-spirited, whatever the merit of the actual complaints. This is particularly important given that recent Iraqi violations have been largely of a technical nature and that the resolution itself is unprecedented in its level of interference in areas traditionally considered the sovereign rights of individual countries. Such violations pale in comparison to those of the aforementioned U.S. allies, whose ongoing military occupations of neighboring countries represent a direct contravention of the UN Charter.

In a similar vein, the United States must support a comprehensive arms control regime for the region, including the establishment of a zone in the Middle East where all weapons of mass destruction are banned. Such an agreement would halt the U.S. practice of bringing nuclear weapons into the region on its planes and ships and would force Israel to dismantle its sizable nuclear arsenal. This more holistic approach to nonproliferation might include, for example, a five-year program affecting not just Iraqi missiles but phasing out Syrian, Israeli, and other missiles as well.

As with its highly selective insistence on the enforcement of UN Security Council resolutions, the double standards in U.S. policy make even the most legitimate concerns about Iraqi weapons development virtually impossible to successfully pursue. If Iraq is truly a threat to regional security, there must be a comprehensive regional security regime worked out between the eight littoral states of the Persian Gulf. The U.S. should support such efforts and not allow its quest for arms sales and oil resources to unnecessarily exacerbate regional tensions.

The United States remains one of the few governments in the world that rejects any linkage between Persian Gulf security issues and Israeli-Palestinian issues. Few people familiar with the region, however, fail to recognize the importance of resolving the Israeli-Palestinian conflict (which would establish a viable Palestinian state with a shared Jerusalem) in order to weaken the appeal and power of demagogues like Saddam Hussein. There is little question of the pivotal role the U.S. plays in the peace process. Washington's failure to force Israeli compromise is the major reason for the current violence and the impasse in negotiations with the Palestinians.

International guarantees protecting the oppressed Kurds of northern Iraq are also necessary. However, they should not be used as an excuse for ongoing punitive air strikes; the Kurds should not yet again be used as pawns in an international rivalry. Comprehensive initiatives for a just settlement of the Kurdish question—including the oppressed Kurdish minority in Turkey and other countries—should be pursued by the international community.

Finally, there needs to be a greater understanding by U.S. policymakers of Iraqi politics and society, which Washington is not only sorely lacking but appears to have done little to improve upon. The reality is that Saddam Hussein will likely remain in power until the Iraqi people are able to overthrow him themselves. An appreciation for how this might best be done could be greatly improved if the United States would be more open to greater dialogue with Iraq's exiled opposition.

In recent years, however, Washington has tended to dismiss input from the Iraqi opposition when crafting U.S. policy toward Iraq.

Although there is nothing inherently wrong with the United States or other countries supporting democratic opposition movements against autocratic regimes, the U.S. has so thoroughly destroyed its credibility that little good can result from actively supporting an Iraqi opposition movement, particularly given its weakness and internal divisions. In particular, support for any kind of military resistance is not only futile but would give the Iraqi regime an excuse to crack down even harder against the country's already-pummeled people. There is little question that, with the lifting of economic sanctions and an end to the bombing, some kind of organized opposition will emerge. However, to be successful, it must be seen as a genuinely indigenous force, not the creation of yet another ill-fated intervention by Western powers.

Twenty Years Later, First Iraq War Still Resonates

The first Persian Gulf War ended on Feb. 28, 1991 — just five days after U.S.-led ground forces first confronted Iraqi troops on Kuwaiti soil, and just over a month after the U.S. had begun bombing Iraq from the air.

It was a short war with a long aftermath.

Then-Iraqi President Saddam Hussein coined a catchphrase when he declared it would be the "mother of all battles" if U.S. and coalition forces sought to eject him from Kuwait. It turned out to be anything but, it was one of history's most lopsided victories on the military side, it turned out not to be the 'mother of all battles' at all."

But the first Gulf War did lead to further confrontations — and its reverberations are still felt today.

Most obviously, it helped set the stage for the U.S.-led invasion of Iraq in 2003. It also became a cause celebre for Osama bin Laden and one of the factors that led to al-Qaida's attacks against the U.S. on Sept. 11, 2001. Bin Laden was incensed that "filthy, infidel crusaders," as he called American troops, were based in his homeland of Saudi Arabia, home to Islam's two holiest sites.

But coming just at the end of the Cold War, Bush was determined that such naked aggression could not be allowed to stand, or no small country would be safe. Bush soon convinced the Saudis that they needed U.S. protection and should provide a staging area for U.S. forces to repel Hussein's forces from Kuwait, unless he pulled out by a Jan. 15 deadline.

Bush won approval of a United Nations resolution allowing such an operation and convinced dozens of countries that they should stand alongside U.S. forces. An air offensive began Jan. 17, seriously softening up Iraqi resolve.

More than half of Iraq's forces had already left Kuwait by the time the coalition's ground offensive began Feb. 24. Despite estimates that Iraq's army — then the fourth largest in the world — would inflict upward of 45,000 casualties, total coalition deaths numbered well under 1,000, according to the Congressional Research Service.

With much — but not all — of Iraq's forces in retreat, U.S. generals liked the idea of ending the ground war on its fifth day, going one better than the Israelis had in their 1967 Six-Day War against neighboring Arab states, according to Bush biographer Herbert Parmet. White House Chief of Staff John Sununu liked the sound of the ground war being completed in

100 hours, so a ceasefire was set for 8 a.m., Riyadh time, on Feb. 28.

Some commanders on the ground were incensed that they were not allowed to decimate more of Iraq's top troops and tanks while they had the chance. Regret would spread during the subsequent weeks, historical accounts suggest.

Before the ground war, Bush had encouraged the Iraqi people to rise up against Hussein, in hopes of staving off a ground invasion. Taking that as encouragement, both Shiites in Iraq's south and Kurds in the north began rebellions after the ceasefire. But they were mowed down within days by the tens of thousands, with Iraq using military helicopters that U.S. commanders allowed them to fly, nominally for the Iraqis' communications purposes.

The U.S. ultimately set up massive operations to help Iraqi refugees and established no-fly zones over northern and southern Iraq to protect their populations. But lasting damage was done to the U.S. image, at least among Shiites in the south.

"One of the impacts was that many Shia in Iraq became very bitter against the U.S.," says James DeFronzo, a University of Connecticut sociologist and author of a book about the second

Iraq war. "That's one of the reasons why, during the second Iraq war, there was not the kind of reception that U.S. soldiers had been led to expect."

U.S. forces would remain in the region, in part to enforce the no-fly zone. This incensed al-Qaida leader Osama bin Laden.

"Bin Laden has repeatedly referred to the U.S. going into Saudi Arabia as a key reason for Sept. 11," says Yetiv, who has just published a history of U.S. policy toward Iraq.

In 1990, Iraq was broke, laden with debt from an eight-year war with Iran that had ended in 1988. That summer, Hussein massed troops along his country's border with Kuwait. Still, U.S. intelligence agencies — along with regional allies such as Saudi Arabia — did not believe Iraq would invade.

Once it did, Iraq won a swift victory, taking control of Kuwait within 12 hours. The great concern among other nations became the threat that Iraq's tanks would then roll into Saudi Arabia, giving Hussein control of a sizable share of the world's oil reserves.

"The stakes in 1990 and '91 were really rather enormous," says Richard Kohn, a military historian at the University of North Carolina. "Had Saddam Hussein gotten control of the Saudi oil fields, he would have had the world economy by the throat. That was immediately recognized by capitals around the world."

Iraq's absorption of Kuwait was initially accepted as a fait accompli, with President George H.W. Bush saying, "There is little the U.S. can do in a situation like this."

Fresh from his symbolically important role in helping to expel the Soviet Union from Afghanistan, bin Laden had been eager to play the leading role in protecting his Saudi homeland from Iraqi incursion.

In September 1990, he told Prince Sultan, the Saudi defense minister, that he could muster 100,000 fighters within three months and there would be no need for American or other "non-Muslim troops."

"There are no caves in Kuwait," Prince Sultan said in response. The Saudis much preferred the promise of hundreds of thousands of Western troops made to them by Dick Cheney, then the U.S. defense secretary, to the prospect of thousands of armed jihadists operating within their borders.

This ultimately led to bin Laden's final break with the Saudi elite and turned his organization's attention toward Western enemies, says Adam Mausner, a research associate at the Center for Strategic and International Studies.

After U.S. forces had remained in Saudi Arabia for some years, bin Laden wrote the Saudi king that "it is unconscionable to let the country become an American colony with American soldiers — their filthy feet everywhere."

"The presence of American troops on Saudi soil galvanized the faction of al-Qaida that wanted to focus on the 'far enemy' first," Mausner says. "Al-Qaida really got on the road to 9/11 because of American troops' presence in Saudi Arabia."

Unfinished Business

Historians of the war have established that no one within the Bush administration argued at the time that coalition forces should exceed the U.N. mandate by chasing Iraqi troops all the way to Baghdad. U.S. officials initially believed that Hussein's regime would fall of its own accord following his loss, but should not be toppled for fear of losing a regional counterweight against Iran.

But Hussein remained a continuing thorn. The U.S. kept up a program of sanctions and bombing through the Clinton years. After the towers fell on Sept. 11, President George W. Bush instructed his advisers to look for connections between Iraq and al-Qaida.Given the threat, the second Bush administration was concerned about the possibility of weapons of mass destruction. Following the 1991 war, weapons inspectors found that Iraq was closer to building nuclear weapons than Western officials had believed, leading to skepticism within the administration when a new round of inspections found no evidence of nuclear weaponry in 2002.

The U.S. invaded Iraq in 2003, with Bush brushing aside warnings from some of his father's advisers that he would face the same trap they had avoided by not going all the way to Baghdad in 1991.Even Wolfowitz, who became a leading advocate for the 2003 invasion as deputy defense secretary, had written in 1997 of that earlier decision that "a new regime would have become a United States responsibility. Conceivably, this could have led the U.S. into a more or less permanent occupation of a country that could not govern itself, but where the rule of a foreign occupier would be increasingly resented."

"It is true that after the end of the war there was a lot of talk about 'Why didn't you finish the job?' " Brent Scowcroft, who served as President George H.W. Bush's national security adviser, said at the Council on Foreign Relations panel.

"And that continued until the second Gulf war," Scowcroft said. "But we don't hear it anymore."

The Gulf War Victory That Never Was

On August 2, 1990, Saddam Hussein, notorious Iraqi strongman, triggered the first great international crisis of the post-Cold War era by invading Kuwait and declaring it Iraq's nineteenth province. With Kuwait in his back pocket and the fourth largest army in the world at his disposal, Saddam effectively controlled two-thirds of the earth's oil reserves, and had every hope of establishing Iraq as the dominant power in the region.

As the Iraqi military build-up continued apace in Kuwait, fears of an invasion of Saudi Arabia mounted. On August 6, George Bush declared, "This will not stand, this aggression of Kuwait," and he meant it. Quickly the American president obtained UN Security Council resolutions condemning the attack, imposing an embargo on Iraq, and seizing its foreign assets.

An extraordinarily diverse military coalition consisting of more than half a million American and 200,000 international troops, including those of key Arab states, was formed under the command of Gen. "Stormin' Norman" Schwarzkopf, and deployed along the Kuwait-Saudi Arabian border over the course of the next several months. The coalition's initial mission, Operation Desert Shield, was to prevent an Iraqi invasion of Saudi Arabia while diplomats, Western and Arab alike, sought to persuade Saddam to withdraw his forces. Its second mission—Operation Desert Storm—was to force Iraq's withdrawal by force of arms if diplomacy failed.

Saddam, believing the United States had no stomach for a conventional war bound to produce heavy casualties in the tinderbox of the Middle East, proved intractable. On the morning of January 17, 1991, phase one of Operation Desert Storm—the air campaign of what the world would soon know as the Persian Gulf War—began.

Desert Storm was the first major test of an all-volunteer U.S. military that had been rebuilt from the ground up following the debacle of Vietnam, and the impact of that experience on the services was everywhere in evidence. From the point of view of doctrine and training, the new American military eschewed protracted and messy insurgencies and inconclusive "operations other than war" in favor of conventional conflicts against regular armies.

The new American military had been kitted out with a welter of new precision-guided weapons, high-tech command-and-control information systems, state-of-the art stealth fighter-bombers, and Abrams tanks that could hit targets 2,500 yards away while traversing rugged terrain in excess of 30 miles an hour with astonishing accuracy.

In short, the new American military possessed a level of speed, mobility, and striking power unprecedented in the history of warfare.

The Generals' War

No battlefield in the history of warfare had been so well prepared for a ground offensive. Before dawn on February 24, the 1st and 2nd Marine Divisions spearheaded the secondary ground attack straight through the middle of the Iraqi forward defenses in southwestern Kuwait, driving relentlessly in the direction of several key oil fields, and Kuwait City itself. The Marines advanced so swiftly through the Iraqi Army's shattered defenses that they encountered only scattered counterattacks, and reached the outskirts of Kuwait City after only two days of fighting. Arab forces were given the honor of liberating the city the next day.

The main ground attack was a massive, "left hook" enveloping maneuver launched from 150 miles west of the Kuwait border in the Saudi Arabian desert by VII Corps, which consisted of 150,000 troops and five heavily armored American and British divisions. After its flanks had been secured by other forces, VII Corps rumbled through the Iraqi desert in the direction of the Rumaila oil fields and Basra, turned sharply to the northeast, and punched hard into the vulnerable right flank of the Iraqi defenses in Kuwait. Its objectives were to cut off the main routes of supply and communication to the Iraqi forces in Kuwait, envelop the elite Republican Guard divisions there, and destroy them.

In the largest armored assault since World War II and the fastest in the history of warfare, coalition forces eviscerated at least ten Iraqi divisions in a mere four days of fighting. In a number of combat engagements, Republican Guard divisions put up fierce resistance, but smoke, rain, and darkness rendered both their commanders and their tankers virtually blind.

Baghdad announced a complete withdrawal of all Iraqi forces from Kuwait on February 26, but coalition forces continued to press the attack until the morning of February 28, when President Bush ordered a cease-fire after only 100 hours of ground combat. The casualty figures reflected the lopsided nature of the fighting: between 25,000 and 65,000 Iraqi soldiers were killed and 75,000 wounded. American losses were 148 killed in action and 467 wounded, while the rest of the coalition suffered 292 killed and 776 wounded.

A cease fire was negotiated on March 3, in which Iraq promised to abide by all UN resolutions.

In the wake of the coalition's lopsided victory, the Bush administration, the media, and defense intellectuals made expansive claims for the war's significance. A wave of patriotism and euphoria swept across the country, the likes of which hadn't been seen since the victories over the Germans and Japanese 45 years earlier.

"Victory in the Gulf leaves us with such feelings of awe," wrote Anthony Lewis, the venerable and urbane New York Times columnist. "By God," declared President Bush, "we've kicked the Vietnam syndrome once and for all."

"This is the end of decline," said Michael Novak of the conservative American Enterprise Institute. "The mother of all battles turned into the daughter of all disasters for the declinists. For years, people are going to cite the lessons of the Persian Gulf." The campaign, said a RAND Corporation study, "constituted a remarkable milestone in military history."

Indeed, the Gulf War heralded an entirely new American way of war, opined a prominent DOD strategist, Andrew Marshall, "in which the information dimension becomes central to the outcome in battles and campaigns. Long-range precision strike weapons coupled to systems of sensors and to command and control systems will fairly soon come to dominate much of warfare."

The victory had indeed finally exorcised the ghosts of Vietnam; a completely recalibrated U.S. military, practicing a new high-tech way of war, had vanquished a brutal dictator and upheld a fundamental principle of international law: thou shalt not invade a sovereign nation's territory. In the first great post-cold war crisis, the U.S. military emerged with enormous prestige. It was widely hailed as the pre-eminent military force in world military history, the mighty Wehrmacht or Roman legions notwithstanding.

That army, with its unprecedented capabilities, would be a vital deterrent to future mischief-making. It would serve as the world community's primary asset in preserving peace and stability in what George H. W. Bush and others referred to as the "New World Order."

Thus, the Persian Gulf War was viewed as a watershed not only in American military history, but in international politics as well.

Yet within a matter of a few months, the bloom began to wear off the rose. Although decapitation of Saddam's Baathist regime had never been a military objective of Desert Storm per se, Washington had ardently hoped that its crushing defeat in the desert would inspire Saddam's overthrow by the Iraqi people, thereby significantly enhancing stability in the region. But the war, it turned out, had been halted too soon. Saddam retained sufficient forces, and then some, to crush brutally two internal uprisings, the Kurds in the north and the Shiites in the south. The American and British air forces had to establish no-fly zones in order to stanch the bloodletting.

What had gone wrong? The Marines' attack on Kuwait City had been meant to tie down the vaunted Republican Guard in combat long enough for the Army's massive left hook to come in behind those elite forces and destroy them. But the Marine thrust had been so devastating and fast that it precipitated the Republican Guard's rapid withdrawal back into Iraq. By the time President Bush had called for a ceasefire to prevent the appearance of unnecessary slaughter—a political rather than a military decision—fully half of the Republican Guard divisions and hundreds of their armored vehicles had escaped deep into Iraq unscathed.

Meanwhile, as the dust settled and cooler heads prevailed in the think tanks and war colleges, it was widely agreed that General Schwarzkopf and his staff had greatly overestimated the capabilities of the enemy. By and large the Iraqi army was creakily obsolescent, poorly led, and brimming over with demoralized conscripts who had deserted their posts en masse rather than stand and fight.

Thus, the splendor of the coalition's victory began to fade, but not sufficiently to stanch the emergence of a new foreign policy consensus among an influential group of civilian intellectuals within the Pentagon, and in the conservative media, that had big things in mind for Greatest Army in World History. With the demise of the Soviet Union, the United States was the world's sole superpower. Indeed, it was the only "indispensable nation."

It had a moral responsibility both to preserve the new world order, and to spread the universal values of freedom, self-determination, and democracy throughout the world. It must punish the enemies of the new order with the help of the world community if possible, but if not, America must be prepared to act unilaterally to do so.

This new creed of military interventionism was hubristic and idealistic at the same time, and drew on a tradition of American exceptionalism as old as Puritan John Winthrop's "City upon a Hill" sermon of 1630. Americans were a unique people, with a special role to play in world affairs.

A cadre of prominent neoconservatives, spearheaded by Robert Kagan, Charles Krauthammer, and William Kristol, spread the gospel of U.S. military intervention as a kind of panacea for all sorts of international problems and crises. "Military strength alone will not avail, counseled Robert Kagan, "if we do not use it actively to maintain a world which both supports and rests on American hegemony."

The Clinton administration embraced the new creed of military interventionism with gusto, as would the Bush administration that followed it. As the Department of Defense Annual Report of 1997 put it, "There is and will continue to be a great need for U.S. forces... not only to protect the United States from direct threats but also to shape the international environment in favorable ways... and to support multinational efforts to ameliorate human suffering and bring peace to the regions torn by ethnic, tribal, or religious conflict.

During the entire Cold War era, there were a total of six major American military deployments. Between 1990 and 1997 alone, U.S. forces conducted operations on foreign shores—peace keeping, peace enforcement, humanitarian relief, traditional combat missions, etc., etc.—more than 30 times, according to Department of Defense sources.

Ironically, the new interventionism completely rejected the Powell doctrine upon which the military had been reconstructed after Vietnam, and the Gulf War had been fought. That doctrine held that if military force was to be used at all, it must be used overwhelmingly, and only in defense of vital national interests, with the full support of the American people, for clearly defined political ends, and with a clear and quick exit strategy.

One of the doctrine's chief objectives was to insure that the military and the nation never again found themselves mired down in another protracted insurgency war with unclear or protean objectives.

As it happened, the much vaunted new world order never materialized, but the new world disorder surely did. Without the built-in constraints imposed by the East-West rivalry, the international community faced a welter of crises from failed and rogue nation states, disgruntled ethnic groups, insurgents and, increasingly in the mid '90s, Islamic terrorism.

American foreign policy decision makers turned to the new American military with unprecedented frequency as a kind of "salvation army," deploying it in places such as Bosnia, Kosovo, Somalia, and Haiti where American interests appeared to be anything but vital, and with decidedly mixed results. Then came 9/11, and the wars in Afghanistan and Iraq. After a period of striking initial success in conventional operations, both wars turned into nightmarish protracted counterinsurgencies that resembled nothing so much as Vietnam.

The most expensive and capable military force in world history found itself completely out of its depth, unable to cope with either the political or military complexities of sectarian guerrilla warfare in cultures it did not understand. Firepower, mass, maneuver, and advanced technologies—the sine qua non of the post-Vietnam American way of war—were hardly the keys to victory against lightly armed insurgents living among the people Americans were meant to protect.

Just after victory in the Persian Gulf in March 1991, a very wise MIT military expert named Barry Posen had cautioned foreign policy decision makers "Don't get the idea it will always be this easy. The terrain was favorable to our high-tech weapons, and we were up against a second-rate gangster. We must not confuse what we did here with using military power to redirect the domestic politics of a society." Neither George W. Bush nor his chief advisors had bothered to listen to Posen, or to a score of other strategists who had carried his message forward into the early 2000s.

And so an entirely new counterinsurgency doctrine for the Army and Marines had to be cobbled together, even as troops en route to the battlefields were rushed through crash counterinsurgency training courses in the California desert. The new field manual, Counterinsurgency, was published in 2006, as U.S. forces struggled to adapt mid-stream to avert defeat in two agonizing and inconclusive conflicts that persist even to this day, albeit under different names.

Notably, the Counterinsurgency field manual instructed American troops to reject many of the tenets, tactics, and ways of thinking that had passed for conventional wisdom about war fighting in the high-tech army of the 1990s and early 2000's. Today, after more than dozen years of continuous combat, the fighting rages on in both Iraq and Afghanistan, and the possibility that substantial American ground forces will once again return to one or both countries is all too real.

After all, these wars are unfinished business, and the new American business, as scholar Andrew Bacevich has eloquently pointed out, is permanent warfare. The Obama administration may have sworn off large deployments for the moment, but in Pakistan, Yemen, and Somalia, "drone attacks employed pursuant to a campaign of targeted assassination [have become] the signature of Obama's new way of war."

Looking back on the post 9/11 perpetual cycle of military operations in his book, The New American Militarism, Bacevich asks, "What has this vast outlay of treasure and this harvest of death and suffering purchased? Simply put, not victory." Meanwhile, the American public's disturbing reaction to this reality, outside the relatively small world of the military itself, has been indifference rather than outrage.

Seen from the vantage point of 2016, the "stunning victory" that was the Gulf War of 1991, that great turning point in American military history and international politics, seems to have lost its former luster. Indeed, the war now appears to have been nothing so much as a lopsided but misleading prequel to the nightmarish civil war in Iraq, and the event that, more than any other, fed the tragic illusion that American military power could and should shape the world environment to fit our imperial will.

The Gulf War Victory That Never Was

Saddam Hussein, notorious Iraqi strongman, triggered the first great international crisis of the post-Cold War era by invading Kuwait and declaring it Iraq's nineteenth province. With Kuwait in his back pocket and the fourth largest army in the world at his disposal, Saddam effectively controlled two-thirds of the earth's oil reserves, and had every hope of establishing Iraq as the dominant power in the region.

As the Iraqi military build-up continued apace in Kuwait, fears of an invasion of Saudi Arabia mounted. On August 6, George Bush declared, "This will not stand, this aggression of Kuwait," and he meant it. Quickly the American president obtained UN Security Council resolutions condemning the attack, imposing an embargo on Iraq, and seizing its foreign assets.

An extraordinarily diverse military coalition consisting of more than half a million American and 200,000 international troops, including those of key Arab states, was formed under the command of Gen. "Stormin' Norman" Schwarzkopf, and deployed along the Kuwait-Saudi Arabian border over the course of the next several months. The coalition's initial mission, Operation Desert Shield, was to prevent an Iraqi invasion of Saudi Arabia while diplomats, Western and Arab alike, sought to persuade Saddam to withdraw his forces. Its second mission—Operation Desert Storm—was to force Iraq's withdrawal by force of arms if diplomacy failed.

Saddam, believing the United States had no stomach for a conventional war bound to produce heavy casualties in the tinderbox of the Middle East, proved intractable. On the morning of January 17, 1991, phase one of Operation Desert Storm—the air campaign of what the world would soon know as the Persian Gulf War—began.

Desert Storm was the first major test of an all-volunteer U.S. military that had been rebuilt from the ground up following the debacle of Vietnam, and the impact of that experience on the services was everywhere in evidence. From the point of view of doctrine and training, the new American military eschewed protracted and messy insurgencies and inconclusive "operations other than war" in favor of conventional conflicts against regular armies.

The new American military had been kitted out with a welter of new precision-guided weapons, high-tech command-and-control information systems, state-of-the art stealth fighter-bombers, and Abrams tanks that could hit targets 2,500 yards away while traversing rugged terrain in excess of 30 miles an hour with astonishing accuracy.

In short, the new American military possessed a level of speed, mobility, and striking power unprecedented in the history of warfare.

The First Gulf War and Its Aftermath

Rise of AL Qaeda

Saddam Hussein, ruler of Iraq, unexpectedly seized Kuwait, capturing it in 48 hours and incorporating it as Iraq's "19th province." American intelligence, believing Iraq exhausted by the recently concluded, decade-long Iran-Iraq war, had expected only posturing or limited aggression from Saddam. Instead, Saddam's invasion would lead to what was then the most massive American military action in the Middle East since WWII.

Indeed, as events unfolded, America's 1990 foray would be followed by an ever-increasing involvement in the region under both Democratic and Republican administrations. In the wake of 1990 would come permanent U.S. basing, and large American forces would remain in the region at levels heretofore only to be found in Europe and East Asia. There would come, as well, multiple and varied uses of American force, which would protect Western interests and some Muslim governments and peoples, but would strike at others. "America," an Iraqi leader would say, "has been bombing my country for 25 years."

Viewed from a quarter century's remove, Saddam's invasion of Kuwait, which seemed so striking and unique at the time, in fact came at a mid-point in four long-running tales of regional dysfunction. In the long run, the unwinding of Saddam's course—an effort, like many, marked by shrewd judgment and error alike—would directly or indirectly affect all four.

The first is the rise of Sunni radicalism, which had begun decades earlier. The second is Iran's quest to preserve its 1979 revolution and spread its radical strain into a Shiite-Islamic empire. The third is the lurching crisis of autocratic misgovernance in the Middle East, a tale with few unblemished heroes since the 1981 assassination of Sadat by Sunni Islamists. To the dysfunction spiraling from the interaction of these three deadly and conflicting forces was added a fourth accelerant, the potential spread of weapons of mass destruction—a Middle Eastern preoccupation since the Israeli destruction of Iraq's Osirak nuclear reactor in 1981.

It might have thus appeared that America's work was now done and that its heightened level of engagement in the region would now recede. Not only had a remarkable coalition been built to defeat Saddam, but pre-war diplomacy had included a measure of U.S.-Soviet cooperation. The U.S.-Soviet rivalry that had required U.S. administrations of both parties to attend closely to regional developments seemed certain to subside. Indeed, within a year the Soviet Union, in another unexpected development, would be gone.

Swept up in this moment and the triumph over Saddam, President Bush and his National Security Adviser Brent Scowcroft decreed a "New World Order." It was to be a world in which nation states would forestall interstate aggression. Justice, administered through joint action under the UN, would reign.

In line with his conceptions, the Bush administration had ended the war abruptly, almost off-handedly, at 100 hours after ground combat began. To preserve his design for the coalition he had built, Bush liberated Kuwait and sued for peace. But Bush had also called for uprisings of oppressed Iraqis and, under advice from government officials, had half-expected Saddam's stunning defeat to lead to his removal. Meanwhile, Scowcroft also planned for Iraq, presumably under new management, quickly to right itself to balance off its neighbor, Iran—in effect hedging New World Order with Old World Realpolitik.

Ever since launching the war on terror in 2001, the United States has struggled to define — let alone defeat — what has proved to be a maddeningly amorphous enemy. Al Qaeda, once a relatively defined and hierarchical group, has metastasized into a multinational movement with franchise operations in at least 16 countries, from Mali to Syria, Yemen to Nigeria. These so-called affiliates have largely replaced the

Pakistan-based mother ship — now known as "al Qaeda core" or "al Qaeda central" — as the driving force of global jihad. That distinction, between the original terrorist group and its offshoots, has recently grown in political significance as U.S. President Barack Obama touts his decimation of al Qaeda's "core leadership" — even if each new start-up renders that victory less and less reassuring.

At all relevant times from in or about 1989 until the date of the filing of this Indictment, an international terrorist group existed which was dedicated to opposing non-Islamic governments with force and violence. This organization grew out of the "mekhtab al khidemat" (the "Services Office") organization which had maintained offices in various parts of the world, including Afghanistan, Pakistan (particularly in Peshawar), and the United States. The group was founded by Usama Bin Laden and Muhammad Atef, a/k/a "Abu Hafs al Masry," together with "Abu Ubaidah al Banshiri," and others. From in or about 1989 until the present, the group called itself "al Qaeda" ("the Base"). From 1989 until in or about 1991, the group (hereafter referred to as "al Qaeda") was headquartered in Afghanistan and Peshawar, Pakistan. In or about 1991, the leadership of al Qaeda, including its "emir" (or prince) Usama Bin Laden, relocated to the Sudan. Al Qaeda was headquartered in the Sudan from approximately 1991 until approximately 1996 but still maintained offices in various parts of the world. In 1996, Usama Bin Laden and other members of al Qaeda relocated to Afghanistan. At all relevant times, al Qaeda was led by its emir, Usama Bin Laden. Members of al Qaeda pledged an oath of allegiance (called a "bayat") to Usama Bin Laden and al Qaeda. Those who were suspected of collaborating against al Qaeda were to be identified and killed.

Bin Laden and al Qaeda violently opposed the United States for several reasons. First, the United States was regarded as an "infidel" because it was not governed in a manner consistent with the group's extremist interpretation of Islam. Second, the United States was viewed as providing essential support for other "infidel" governments and institutions, particularly the governments of Saudi Arabia and Egypt, the nation of Israel, and the United Nations organization, which were regarded as enemies of the group. Third, al Qaeda opposed the involvement of the United States armed forces in the Gulf War in 1991 and in Operation Restore Hope in Somalia in 1992 and 1993. In particular, al Qaeda opposed the continued presence of American military forces in Saudi Arabia (and elsewhere on the Saudi Arabian peninsula) following the Gulf War. Fourth, al Qaeda opposed the United States Government because of the arrest, conviction and imprisonment of persons belonging to al Qaeda or its affiliated terrorist groups or those with whom it worked. For these and other reasons, Bin Laden declared a jihad, or holy war, against the United States, which he has carried out through al Qaeda and its affiliated organizations.

One of the principal goals of al Qaeda was to drive the United States armed forces out of Saudi Arabia (and elsewhere on the Saudi Arabian peninsula) and Somalia by violence. Members of al Qaeda issued fatwahs (rulings on Islamic law) indicating that such attacks were both proper and necessary.

Usama Bin Laden and al Qaeda also forged alliances with the National Islamic Front in the Sudan and with representatives of the government of Iran, and its associated terrorist group Hizballah, for the purpose of working together against their perceived common enemies in the West, particularly the United States.

Since at least 1989, until the filing of this Indictment, Usama Bin Laden and the terrorist group al Qaeda sponsored, managed, and/or financially supported training camps in Afghanistan, which camps were used to instruct members and associates of al Qaeda and its affiliated terrorist groups in the use of firearms, explosives, chemical weapons, and other weapons of mass destruction. In addition to providing training in the use of various weapons, these camps were used to conduct operational planning against United States targets around the world and experiments in the use of chemical and biological weapons. These camps were also used to train others in security and counterintelligence methods, such as the use of codes and passwords, and to teach members and associates of al Qaeda about traveling to perform operations. For example, al Qaeda instructed its members and associates to dress in "Western" attire and to use other methods to avoid detection by security officials. The group also taught its members and associates to monitor media reporting of its operations to determine the effectiveness of their terrorist activities.

In furtherance of the conspiracy, and to affect its objects, the defendant, and others known and unknown to the Grand Jury, committed the following overt acts:

The Provision of Guesthouses and Training Camps

At various times from at least as early as 1989, Usama Bin Laden, and others known and unknown, provided training camps and guesthouses in Afghanistan, including camps known as Khalden, Derunta, Khost, Siddiq, and Jihad Wal, for the use of al Qaeda and its affiliated groups.

In 1990, unindicted co-conspirators, known and unknown, provided military and intelligence training in various areas, including Afghanistan, Pakistan, and the Sudan, for the use of al Qaeda and its affiliated groups, including the Egyptian Islamic Jihad.

Usama Bin Laden, and others known and unknown, engaged in financial and business transactions on behalf of al Qaeda, including, but not limited to: purchasing land for training camps; purchasing warehouses for storage of items, including explosives; purchasing communications and electronics equipment; transferring funds between corporate accounts; and transporting currency and weapons to members of al Qaeda and its associated terrorist organizations in various countries throughout the world.

The Efforts to Obtain Nuclear Weapons and Their Components

Usama Bin Laden, and others known and unknown, made efforts to obtain the components of nuclear weapons.

The Fatwahs Against American Troops in Saudi Arabia and Yemen until the date of the filing of this Indictment, Usama Bin Laden, working together with members of the fatwah committee of al Qaeda, disseminated fatwahs to other members and associates of al Qaeda that the United States forces stationed on the Saudi Arabian peninsula, including both Saudi Arabia and Yemen, should be attacked or about 1993, Usama Bin Laden, working together with members of the fatwah committee of al Qaeda, disseminated fatwahs to other members and associates of al Qaeda that the United States forces stationed in the Horn of Africa, including Somalia, should be attacked.

The Fatwah Regarding Deaths of Nonbelievers

An unindicted co-conspirator advised other members of al Qaeda that it was Islamic ally proper to engage in violent actions against "infidels" (nonbelievers), even if others might be killed by such actions, because if the others were "innocent," they would go to paradise, and if they were not "innocent," they deserved to die.

Declaration of Jihad indicating that it was from the Hindu Kush mountains in Afghanistan entitled, "Message from Usamah Bin-Muhammad Bin-Laden to His Muslim Brothers in the Whole World and Especially in the Arabian Peninsula: Declaration of Jihad Against the Americans Occupying the Land of the Two Holy Mosques; Expel the Heretics from the Arabian Peninsula" was disseminated.

Usama Bin Laden endorsed a fatwah under the banner of the "International Islamic Front for Jihad on the Jews and Crusaders." This fatwah, published in the publication Al-Quds al-'Arabi on February 23, 1998, stated that Muslims should kill Americans including civilians anywhere in the world where they can be found. Usama Bin Laden cited American aggression against Islam and encouraged a jihad that would eliminate the Americans from the Arabian Peninsula.

Usama Bin Laden issued a statement entitled "The Nuclear Bomb of Islam," under the banner of the "International Islamic Front for Fighting the Jews and the Crusaders," in which he stated that "it is the duty of the Muslims to prepare as much force as possible to terrorize the enemies of God."

Usama Bin Laden called for a "jihad" to release the "brothers" in jail "everywhere."

How the US Helped Create Al Qaeda and ISIS

Much like Al Qaeda, the Islamic State (ISIS) is made-in-the-USA, an instrument of terror designed to divide and conquer the oil-rich Middle East and to counter Iran's growing influence in the region.

The fact that the United States has a long and torrid history of backing terrorist groups will surprise only those who watch the news and ignore history.

The CIA first aligned itself with extremist Islam during the Cold War era. Back then, America saw the world in rather simple terms: on one side, the Soviet Union and Third World nationalism, which America regarded as a Soviet tool; on the other side, Western nations and militant political Islam, which America considered an ally in the struggle against the Soviet Union.

The director of the National Security Agency under Ronald Reagan, General William Odom recently remarked, "by any measure the U.S. has long used terrorism. In 1978-79 the Senate was trying to pass a law against international terrorism – in every version they produced, the lawyers said the U.S. would be in violation."

During the 1970's the CIA used the Muslim Brotherhood in Egypt as a barrier, both to thwart Soviet expansion and prevent the spread of Marxist ideology among the Arab masses. The United States also openly supported Sarekat Islam against Sukarno in Indonesia, and supported the Jamaat-e-Islami terror group against Zulfiqar Ali Bhutto in Pakistan. Last but certainly not least, there is Al Qaeda.

Lest we forget, the CIA gave birth to Osama Bin Laden and breastfed his organization during the 1980's. Former British Foreign Secretary, Robin Cook, told the House of Commons that Al Qaeda was unquestionably a product of Western intelligence agencies. Mr. Cook explained that Al Qaeda, which literally means an abbreviation of "the database" in Arabic, was originally the computer database of the thousands of Islamist extremists, who were trained by the CIA and funded by the Saudis, in order to defeat the Russians in Afghanistan.

America's relationship with Al Qaeda has always been a love-hate affair. Depending on whether a particular Al Qaeda terrorist group in a given region furthers American interests or not, the U.S. State Department either funds or aggressively targets that terrorist group. Even as American foreign policy makers claim to oppose Muslim extremism, they knowingly foment it as a weapon of foreign policy.

The Islamic State is its latest weapon that, much like Al Qaeda, is certainly backfiring. ISIS recently rose to international prominence after its thugs began beheading American journalists. Now the terrorist group controls an area the size of the United Kingdom.

HOW THE BUSH WARS OPENED THE DOOR FOR ISIS

It's been a long quarter-century since the first President Bush put the U.S. on the road to an Iraq-Afghanistan quagmire. It's been barely a year since ISIS became a national obsession.

In order to understand why the Islamic State has grown and flourished so quickly, one has to take a look at the organization's American-backed roots. The 2003 American invasion and occupation of Iraq created the pre-conditions for radical Sunni groups, like ISIS, to take root. America, rather unwisely, destroyed Saddam Hussein's secular state machinery and replaced it with a predominantly Shiite administration. The U.S. occupation caused vast unemployment in Sunni areas, by rejecting socialism and closing down factories in the naive hope that the magical hand of the free market would create jobs. Under the new U.S.-backed Shiite regime, working class Sunni's lost hundreds of thousands of jobs. Unlike the white Afrikaners in South Africa, who were allowed to keep their wealth after regime change, upper class Sunni's were systematically dispossessed of their assets and lost their political influence. Rather than promoting religious integration and unity, American policy in Iraq exacerbated sectarian divisions and created a fertile breading ground for Sunni discontent, from which Al Qaeda in Iraq took root.

The Islamic State of Iraq and Syria (ISIS) used to have a different name: Al Qaeda in Iraq. After 2010 the group rebranded and refocused its efforts on Syria.

There are essentially three wars being waged in Syria: one between the government and the rebels, another between Iran and Saudi Arabia, and yet another between America and Russia. It is this third, neo-Cold War battle that made U.S. foreign policy makers decide to take the risk of arming Islamist rebels in Syria, because Syrian President, Bashar al-Assad, is a key Russian ally. Rather embarrassingly, many of these Syrian rebels have now turned out to be ISIS thugs, who are openly brandishing American-made M16 Assault rifles.

America's Middle East policy revolves around oil and Israel. The invasion of Iraq has partially satisfied Washington's thirst for oil, but ongoing air strikes in Syria and economic sanctions on Iran have everything to do with Israel. The goal is to deprive Israel's neighboring enemies, Lebanon's Hezbollah and Palestine's Hamas, of crucial Syrian and Iranian support.

ISIS is not merely an instrument of terror used by America to topple the Syrian government; it is also used to put pressure on Iran.

The last time Iran invaded another nation was in 1738. Since independence in 1776, the U.S. has been engaged in over 53 military invasions and expeditions. Despite what the Western media's war cries would have you believe, Iran is clearly not the threat to regional security, Washington is. An Intelligence Report published in 2012, endorsed by all sixteen U.S. intelligence agencies, confirms that Iran ended its nuclear weapons program in 2003. Truth is, any Iranian nuclear ambition, real or imagined, is as a result of American hostility towards Iran, and not the other way around.

America is using ISIS in three ways: to attack its enemies in the Middle East, to serve as a pretext for U.S. military intervention abroad, and at home to foment a manufactured domestic threat, used to justify the unprecedented expansion of invasive domestic surveillance.

By rapidly increasing both government secrecy and surveillance, Mr. Obama's government is increasing its power to watch its citizens, while diminishing its citizens' power to watch their government. Terrorism is an excuse to justify mass surveillance, in preparation for mass revolt.

The so-called "War on Terror" should be seen for what it really is: a pretext for maintaining a dangerously oversized U.S. military. The two most powerful groups in the U.S. foreign policy establishment are the Israel lobby, which directs U.S. Middle East policy, and the Military-Industrial-Complex, which profits from the former group's actions. Since George W. Bush declared the "War on Terror" in October 2001, it has cost the American taxpayer approximately 6.6 trillion dollars and thousands of fallen sons and daughters; but, the wars have also raked in billions of dollars for Washington's military elite.

In 1997, a U.S. Department of Defense report stated, "the data show a strong correlation between U.S. involvement abroad and an increase in terrorist attacks against the U.S." Truth is, the only way America can win the "War On Terror" is if it stops giving terrorists the motivation and the resources to attack America. Terrorism is the symptom; American imperialism in the Middle East is the cancer. Put simply, the War on Terror is terrorism; only, it is conducted on a much larger scale by people with jets and missiles.

It has been an unbelievable 25 years since George H. W. Bush started us on the adventure that still isn't over in Iraq and Afghanistan. There are American soldiers fighting and dying in the Middle East right now who weren't even born when Bush the Elder declared the Iraqi invasion and occupation of Kuwait to be an intolerable situation and sent roughly half a million Americans halfway around the world to reverse it.

Twenty-five years down the road is not a bad moment to stop and ask,what the heck was that all about? And what did we accomplish for our pains, especially the sacrifices of individual American soldiers? We now say "Thank you for your service" to anyone in a military uniform. This is a nice new civic custom that hasn't, to my surprise, turned into an interest-group free-for-all. What about policemen? And firemen? Or the immigrants who keep Southern California shiny? Aren't we grateful to them for their service? Sure, but we recognize that the military is different, and special. And I've never understood how it honors dead and wounded troops to perpetuate mistaken wars, in which their numbers can only increase.

Who is Isis? The rise of the Islamic State in Iraq and the Levant

With its multi-pronged assault across central and northern Iraq in the past one and a half weeks, the Islamic State of Iraq and the Levant (Isis) has taken over from the al-Qa'ida organisation founded by Osama bin Laden as the most powerful and effective extreme jihadi group in the world.

Isis now controls or can operate with impunity in a great stretch of territory in western Iraq and eastern Syria, making it militarily the most successful jihadi movement ever.

While its exact size is unclear, the group is thought to include thousands of fighters. The last "s" of "Isis" comes from the Arabic word "al-Sham", meaning Levant, Syria or occasionally Damascus, depending on the circumstances.

Led since 2010 by Abu Bakr al-Baghdadi, also known as Abu Dua (see below), it has proved itself even more violent and sectarian than what US officials call the "core" al-Qa'ida, led by Ayman al-Zawahiri, who is based in Pakistan.

Isis is highly fanatical, killing Shia Muslims and Christians whenever possible, as well as militarily efficient and under tight direction by top leaders.

The creation of a sort of proto-Caliphate by extreme jihadis in northern Syria and Iraq is provoking fears in surrounding countries such as Jordan, Saudi Arabia and Turkey that they will become targets of battle-hardened Sunni fighters.

The Isis tactic is to make a surprise attack, inflict maximum casualties and spread fear before withdrawing without suffering heavy losses. Last Friday they attacked Mosul, where their power is already strong enough to tax local businesses, from family groceries to mobile phone and construction companies. Some 200 people were killed in the fighting, according to local hospitals, though the government gives a figure of 59 dead, 21 of them policemen and 38 insurgents.

Isis specialises in using militarily untrained foreign volunteers as suicide bombers either moving on foot wearing suicide vests, or driving vehicles packed with explosives. Often more than one suicide bomber is used, as happened when a vehicle exploded at the headquarters of a Kurdish party, the Patriotic Union of Kurdistan in the town of Jalawla in the divided and much fought-over province of Diyala, north-east of Baghdad. In the confusion caused by the blast, a second bomber on foot slipped into the office and blew himself up, killing some 18 people, including a senior police officer.

The swift rise of Isis since Abu Bakr al-Baghdadi became its leader has come because the uprising of the Sunni in Syria in 2011 led the Iraqi Sunni to protest about their political and economic marginalisation since the fall of Saddam Hussein. Peaceful demonstrations from the end of 2012 won few concessions, with Iraq's Shia-dominated government convinced that the protesters wanted not reform but a revolution returning their community to power. The five or six million Iraqi Sunni became more alienated and sympathetic towards armed action by Isis. Isis launched a well-planned campaign last year including a successful assault on Abu Ghraib prison last summer to free leaders and experienced fighters. This January, they took over Fallujah, 40 miles west of Baghdad, and have held it ever since in the face of artillery and air attack. The military sophistication of Isis in Iraq is much greater than al-Qa'ida, the organisation out of which it grew, which reached the peak of its success in 2006-07 before the Americans turned many of the Sunni tribes against it. Isis has the great advantage of being able to operate on both sides of the Syrian-Iraq border, though in Syria it is engaged in an intra-jihadi civil war with Jabhat al-Nusra, Ahrar al-Sham and other groups. But Isis controls Raqqa, the only provincial capital taken by the opposition, and much of eastern Syria outside enclaves held by the Kurds close to the Turkish border.

Isis is today a little more circumspect in killing all who work for the government including rubbish collectors, something that alienated the Sunni population previously. But horrifically violent, though professionally made propaganda videos show Isis forcing families with sons in the Iraqi army to dig their own graves before they are shot. The message is that their enemies can expect no mercy.

Who is Isis leader Abu Bakr al-Baghdadi?

An undated picture released by Iraq's Interior Ministry claiming to show Isis leader Abu Bakr al-Baghdadi.

In the space of a year he has become the most powerful jihadi leader in the world, and last week his forces captured Mosul, the northern capital of Iraq. Abu Bakr al-Baghdadi, also known as Abu Dua, the leader of the Islamic State of Iraq and the Levant (Isis) has suddenly emerged as a figure who is shaping the future of Iraq, Syria and the wider Middle East.

He began to appear from the shadows in the summer of 2010 when he became leader of al-Qa'ida in Iraq (AQI) after its former leaders were killed in an attack by US and Iraqi troops. AQI was at a low point in its fortunes, as the Sunni rebellion, in which it had once played a leading role, was collapsing. It was revived by the revolt of the Sunni in Syria in 2011 and, over the next three years by a series of carefully planned campaigns in both Iraq and Syria. How far al-Baghdadi is directly responsible for the military strategy and tactics of Isis, once called AQI, is uncertain: former Iraqi army and intelligence officers from the Saddam era are said to play a crucial role, but are under al-Baghdadi's overall leadership.

There are disputes over his career depending on whether the source is Isis itself, US or Iraqi intelligence but the overall picture appears fairly clear. He was born in Samarra, a largely Sunni city north of Baghdad, in 1971 and is well educated. With black hair and brown eyes, a picture of al-Baghdadi taken when he was a prisoner of the Americans in Bocca Camp in southern Iraq between 2005 and 2009, makes him look like any Iraqi man in his thirties.

His real name is believed to be Awwad Ibrahim Ali al-Badri al-Samarrai, who has degrees in Islamic Studies, including poetry, history and genealogy, from the Islamic University of Baghdad. He may have been an Islamic militant under Saddam as a preacher in Diyala province, to the north east of Baghdad, where, after the US invasion of 2003, he had his own armed group. Insurgent movements have a strong motive for giving out misleading information about their command structure and leadership, but it appears al-Baghdadi spent five years as prisoner of the Americans.

After the old AQI leadership was killed in April 2010, al-Baghdadi took over and AQI became increasingly well organised, even issuing detailed annual reports over the last two years, itemising its operations in each Iraqi province. Recalling the fate of his predecessors as AQI leader, he insisted on extreme secrecy, so few people knew where he was. AQI prisoners either say they have never met him or, when they did, that he was wearing a mask.

Taking advantage of the Syrian civil war, al-Baghdadi sent experienced fighters and funds to Syria to set up Jabhat al-Nusra as al-Qa'ida's affiliate in Syria. He split from it last year, but remains in control of a great swathe of territory in northern Syria and Iraq. Against fragmented and dysfunctional opposition, he is moving fast towards establishing himself as Emir of a new Islamic state.

Where we stand today

ISIS considers itself the "Islamic Caliphate" (a theological empire) and controls vast swathes of land in western Iraq and eastern Syria. They also have "allegiance" from different radical Islamic groups around the world (from Afghanistan to Nigeria) who "govern" self-proclaimed provinces.

Within the areas they control they have established a reign of terror second to none. They have institutionalized slavery and rape (particularly of adherents to the Yazidi religion who they view as devil worshippers) and have carried out genocide and ethnic cleansing of Christians, Alawites, and other Shiites and Yazidis in the territories they control.

They have struck with a vengeance beyond their territories. Suicide attacks in Baghdad, Beirut, and Ankara killed hundreds. In October 2015, they detonated a bomb aboard a

Russian airliner leaving from Sharm el-Sheikh airport in Egypt, killing all 224 people on board. In November, they orchestrated a multi-suicide attack in Paris, killing 129 people. They have inspired "lone-wolf" terror attacks by sympathizers in places as far away as Ottawa and Sydney.

ISIS referred to as IS, ISIL, or Daesh. All of these acronyms describe the group in question. Islamic State of Iraq and Syria was the name of the group when it captured Mosul in 2014 and became the terrorist juggernaut it is today. They named themselves that to assert their dominance in Syria .

Islamic State of Iraq and the Levant (aka Greater Syria) is the name that Obama uses to describe the group (pretty much only Obama uses it). Superficially speaking, it is just a translation thing.

Islamic State is the name the group gave itself after a "rebranding" effort when they wanted to show off their global strategy (they wouldn't be limited to Syria and Iraq anymore).

Daesh is essentially the Arabic acronym of the group. People assume that using this word somehow weakens them... it doesn't, because unfortunately in this case it is one of those "sticks and stones" things.

ISIS was born out of the U.S. invasion of Iraq in 2003. When U.S. administrators, under Paul Bremer, decided to "de-

Baathify" the Iraqi civil and military services, hundreds of thousands of Sunnis formerly loyal to Saddam Hussein were left without a job — and they were mad. Al Qaeda chose to capitalize on their anger and established al Qaeda in Iraq (AQI) to wage an insurgency against U.S. troops in Iraq (Saddam was secular, but his intelligence and military supporters were able to make common cause with the jihadis of al Qaeda).

During this time they were quite active in waging a sectarian war against Iran-backed Shiite militias in central Iraq and bombing hotels in neighboring Jordan. Many of their members were imprisoned in U.S.-run "Camp Bucca," where they were able to meet up and radicalize.

Fast forward to the U.S. "surge" in 2007: The U.S.-installed, Shiite government in Baghdad began reaching out to Sunni tribes, encouraging them to reject AQI. By this point, AQI was basically defeated and it looked like peace was coming to the Middle East .

Fast forward again to the Arab Spring and the uprising against Syrian dictator Bashar al-Assad .During the Iraq War, AQI would frequently go back and forth between Syria and Iraq to resupply, so it had a lot of contacts in the country. When Assad began shooting and gassing his own people, and the peaceful uprising turned into a civil war, AQI saw an opportunity to establish a presence there.

It quickly moved into Syria, renamed itself as The Islamic State of Iraq and Syria (ISIS), and merged with its Syrian counterpart. This pissed off al Qaeda's HQ, because they were already establishing a separate al Qaeda in Syria (aka al-Nusra front) and wanted it to remain separate. The two groups fought another mini-war amongst themselves and officially separated with AQI rebranding itself into the ISIS we hear about today.

It is important to note that this tiff between the two groups was global and concerned some "practical" things (like if al Qaeda should rule territory or kill Sunnis), as well as ego matters (like if Osama Bin Laden's lieutenants, who have been on the run since 2001, should be the ones calling the shots). The intra-jihadi battle was waged on the battlefields of Syria, Iraq, Somalia, and northwest Africa, as well as in jihadi forums on the dark net.

As the Syrian civil war ground on, ISIS became the first rebel group to capture major cities (Raqqa and Deir ez-Zor). In the summer of 2014, the group had its breakout moment. In a lightning offensive, it captured Mosul in Iraq and drove south until it was on the borders of Baghdad. A few weeks later it rebranded itself as a Caliphate and demanded that all Muslims pledge allegiance (bay'ah). At this point, groups like Boko Haram in Nigeria and Ansar Beit Al Maqdis in Egypt's

Sinai began pledging allegiance and flew the black flag of ISIS. They also established presences in half a dozen other countries.

ISIS grew in notoriety through an aggressive social media and viral video strategy that had it engage with sympathizers and glorify violence. It beheaded many of its victims, including U.S. journalist James Foley. It often filmed executions through drowning, burning alive, and shooting. When it captured the northern Iraqi town of Sinjar, it institutionalized slavery and rape of the Yazidi minority. In short, it installed a reign of barbaric terror.

How did ISIS grow to become so powerful?

Born of the Iraqi and Syrian civil wars, the Islamic State astonished the world in 2014 by creating a powerful new force in the Middle East. By combining religious fanaticism and military prowess, the new self-declared caliphate poses a threat to the political status quo of the whole region.

There are a number of forces that can explain its strength.

Feelings of disenfranchisement:

Sunni communities in Iraq and Syria felt alienated by Shiite- and Alawite-led governments. ISIS played on these feelings, pushing forward a sense of victimhood and giving these communities a means to feel in control through violence. They also advanced a twisted interpretation of Islam that found ripe fodder among disenfranchised youth in the area.

Unlikely bedfellows:

ISIS partnered with the lieutenants of Saddam Hussein's secular regime (who used to hate jihadis) to perfect their tools of repression along the same lines that Saddam used.

Syrian chaos:

There is little doubt that as U.S. allies (Saudi Arabia, Qatar ,and Turkey) ploughed money and arms into the Syrian civil war much of it ended up in the hands of ISIS (and other jihadi groups).

<u>Iraqi chaos:</u>

After the U.S. withdrawal from Iraq, the atrophied Iraqi army was over-equipped and underprepared (and very corrupt) to deal with ISIS. Much of the weaponry ended up in ISIS's hands.

Racketeering and extortion: Before ISIS formally controlled Mosul, it would run a racketeering business (similar to that used by the U.S. mafia) under the nose of the Iraqi government. Businesses and individuals had to pay them a "protection fee" to stay safe.

<u>Taxation and exploitation:</u>

Properties belonging to religious minorities or regime sympathizers were promptly appropriated (e.g. churches, gold, hard currency), and once ISIS controlled territory and people it began taxing them like any state would.

<u>Selling oil:</u>

It is the Middle East, so oil is always involved. While technically shut out from the international markets, ISIS could and did still find markets for its oil (usually in neighboring Turkey whose government was sympathetic to many of the Syrian jihadis).

So what now?

There are about a dozen countries (some of which hate each other) fighting ISIS. All of them (except for Iran, Syria, and Iraq) are basically doing it by bombing them from the sky. The U.S. has committed a few hundred "advisors" to the fight (and they are most certainly not wearing boots).

Despite a yearlong campaign against ISIS, the group still controls a lot of territory (even capturing new ground like Palmyra in Syria) and has demonstrated that it can strike in the heart of the Western world.

Post-Paris, there seems to be growing momentum for ground troop involvement against ISIS. The Obama administration has remained reluctant, insisting that its strategy is the successful one and that ISIS is weaker now than before. Syrian President Bashar al-Assad feels emboldened with Russia and Iran by his side, knowing that it is less likely for the West to oust him if the alternative will be ISIS.

As the Syrian civil war closes its fifth year, ISIS seems stronger than ever and the refugee exodus does not look like it will end. As Western governments try to grapple with the threat of ISIS terror reaching the Western world, they will feel the pressure to lock out these refugees (who are also fleeing ISIS). By using refugees as a convenient scapegoat, the risk is alienating them, leaving them susceptible to the toxic mix of conspiracy theories and extremism that breeds jihadi violence.

It should go without saying that while ISIS is a radical Islamic group/movement, it does not, by any means, represent the views of the vast majority of Muslims. The majority of its victims have been Muslims and its twisted interpretation of the Koran is not shared by the 1 billion+ adherents of the Muslim faith.

ISIS Enshrines a Theology of Rape

Claiming the Quran's support, the Islamic State codifies sex slavery in conquered regions of Iraq and Syria and uses the practice as a recruiting tool.

In the moments before he raped the 12-year-old girl, the Islamic State fighter took the time to explain that what he was about to do was not a sin. Because the preteen girl practiced a religion other than Islam, the Quran not only gave him the right to rape her — it condoned and encouraged it, he insisted.

He bound her hands and gagged her. Then he knelt beside the bed and prostrated himself in prayer before getting on top of her.

When it was over, he knelt to pray again, bookending the rape with acts of religious devotion.

"I kept telling him it hurts — please stop," said the girl, whose body is so small an adult could circle her waist with two hands. "He told me that according to Islam he is allowed to rape an unbeliever. He said that by raping me, he is drawing closer to God," she said in an interview alongside her family in a refugee camp here, to which she escaped after 11 months of captivity. The systematic rape of women and girls from the Yazidi religious minority has become deeply enmeshed in the organization and the radical theology of the Islamic State in the year since the group announced it was reviving slavery as an institution. Interviews with 21 women and girls who recently escaped the Islamic State, as well as an examination of the group's official communications, illuminate how the practice has been enshrined in the group's core tenets.

The trade in Yazidi women and girls has created a persistent infrastructure, with a network of warehouses where the victims are held, viewing rooms where they are inspected and marketed, and a dedicated fleet of buses used to transport them.

A total of 5,270 Yazidis were abducted last year, and at least 3,144 are still being held, according to community leaders. To handle them, the Islamic State has developed a detailed bureaucracy of sex slavery, including sales contracts notarized by the ISIS-run Islamic courts. And the practice has become an established recruiting tool to lure men from deeply conservative Muslim societies, where casual sex is taboo and dating is forbidden.

A growing body of internal policy memos and theological discussions has established guidelines for slavery, including a lengthy how-to manual issued by the Islamic State Research and Fatwa Department just last month. Repeatedly, the ISIS leadership has emphasized a narrow and selective reading of the Quran and other religious rulings to not only justify violence, but also to elevate and celebrate each sexual assault as spiritually beneficial, even virtuous.

"Every time that he came to rape me, he would pray," said F, a 15-year-old girl who was captured on the shoulder of Mount Sinjar one year ago and was sold to an Iraqi fighter in his 20s. Like some others interviewed by The New York Times, she wanted to be identified only by her first initial because of the shame associated with rape.

"He kept telling me this is ibadah," she said, using a term from Islamic scripture meaning worship.

"He said that raping me is his prayer to God. I said to him, 'What you're doing to me is wrong, and it will not bring you closer to God.' And he said, 'No, it's allowed. It's halal,' " said the teenager, who escaped in April with the help of smugglers after being enslaved for nearly nine months.

Calculated Conquest

The Islamic State's formal introduction of systematic sexual slavery dates to Aug. 3, 2014, when its fighters invaded the villages on the southern flank of Mount Sinjar, a craggy massif of dun-colored rock in northern Iraq.

Its valleys and ravines are home to the Yazidis, a tiny religious minority who represent less than 1.5 percent of Iraq's estimated population of 34 million.

The offensive on the mountain came just two months after the fall of Mosul, the second-largest city in Iraq. At first, it appeared that the subsequent advance on the mountain was just another attempt to extend the territory controlled by Islamic State fighters.

Almost immediately, there were signs that their aim this time was different.

Survivors say that men and women were separated within the first hour of their capture. Adolescent boys were told to lift up their shirts, and if they had armpit hair, they were directed to join their older brothers and fathers. In village after village, the men and older boys were driven or marched to nearby fields, where they were forced to lie down in the dirt and sprayed with automatic fire.

The women, girls and children, however, were hauled off in open-bed trucks.

"The offensive on the mountain was as much a sexual conquest as it was for territorial gain," said Matthew Barber, a University of Chicago expert on the Yazidi minority. He was in Dohuk, near Mount Sinjar, when the onslaught began last summer and helped create a foundation that provides psychological support for the escapees, who number more than 2,000, according to community activists.

Fifteen-year-old F says her family of nine was trying to escape, speeding up mountain switchbacks, when their aging Opel overheated. She, her mother, and her sisters — 14, 7, and 4 years old — were helplessly standing by their stalled car when a convoy of heavily armed Islamic State fighters encircled them.

"Right away, the fighters separated the men from the women," she said. She, her mother and sisters were first taken in trucks to the nearest town on Mount Sinjar. "There, they separated me from my mom. The young, unmarried girls were forced to get into buses."

The buses were white, with a painted stripe next to the word "Hajj," suggesting that the Islamic State had commandeered Iraqi government buses used to transport pilgrims for the annual pilgrimage to Mecca. So many Yazidi women and girls were loaded inside F's bus that they were forced to sit on each other's laps, she said.

Once the bus headed out, they noticed that the windows were blocked with curtains, an accouterment that appeared to have been added because the fighters planned to transport large numbers of women who were not covered in burqas or head scarves.

F's account, including the physical description of the bus, the placement of the curtains and the manner in which the women were transported, is echoed by a dozen other female victims interviewed for this article. They described a similar set of circumstances even though they were kidnapped on different days and in locations miles apart.

F says she was driven to the Iraqi city of Mosul some six hours away, where they herded them into the Galaxy Wedding Hall. Other groups of women and girls were taken to a palace from the Saddam Hussein era, the Badoosh prison compound and the Directory of Youth building in Mosul, recent escapees said. And in addition to Mosul, women were herded into elementary schools and municipal buildings in the Iraqi towns of Tal Afar, Solah, Ba'aj and Sinjar City.

They would be held in confinement, some for days, some for months. Then, inevitably, they were loaded into the same fleet of buses again before being sent in smaller groups to Syria or to other locations inside Iraq, where they were bought and sold for sex.

"It was 100 percent preplanned," said Khider Domle, a Yazidi community activist who maintains a detailed database of the victims. "I spoke by telephone to the first family who arrived at the Directory of Youth in Mosul, and the hall was already prepared for them. They had mattresses, plates and utensils, food and water for hundreds of people."

Detailed reports by Human Rights Watch and Amnesty International reach the same conclusion about the organized nature of the sex trade.

In each location, survivors say Islamic State fighters first conducted a census of their female captives.

Inside the voluminous Galaxy banquet hall, F sat on the marble floor, squeezed between other adolescent girls. In all she estimates there were over 1,300 Yazidi girls sitting, crouching, splayed out and leaning against the walls of the ballroom, a number that is confirmed by several other women held in the same location.They each described how three Islamic State fighters walked in, holding a register. They told the girls to stand. Each one was instructed to state her first, middle and last name, her age, her hometown, whether she was married, and if she had children.

For two months, F was held inside the Galaxy hall. Then one day, they came and began removing young women. Those who refused were dragged out by their hair, she said.

In the parking lot the same fleet of Hajj buses was waiting to take them to their next destination, said F. Along with 24 other girls and young women, the 15-year-old was driven to an army base in Iraq. It was there in the parking lot that she heard the word "sabaya" for the first time.

"They laughed and jeered at us, saying 'You are our sabaya.' I didn't know what that word meant," she said. Later on, the local Islamic State leader explained it meant slave.

"He told us that Taus Malik" — one of seven angels to whom the Yazidis pray — "is not God. He said that Taus Malik is the devil and that because you worship the devil, you belong to us. We can sell you and use you as we see fit."

The Islamic State's sex trade appears to be based solely on enslaving women and girls from the Yazidi minority. As yet, there has been no widespread campaign aimed at enslaving women from other religious minorities, said Samer Muscati, the author of the recent Human Rights Watch report. That assertion was echoed by community leaders, government officials and other human rights workers.

Mr. Barber, of the University of Chicago, said that the focus on Yazidis was likely because they are seen as polytheists, with an oral tradition rather than a written scripture. In the Islamic State's eyes that puts them on the fringe of despised unbelievers, even more than Christians and Jews, who are considered to have some limited protections under the Quran as "People of the Book."

In Kojo, one of the southernmost villages on Mount Sinjar and among the farthest away from escape, residents decided to stay, believing they would be treated as the Christians of

Mosul had months earlier. On Aug. 15, 2014, the Islamic State ordered the residents to report to a school in the center of town.

When she got there, 40-year-old Aishan Ali Saleh found a community elder negotiating with the Islamic State, asking if they could be allowed to hand over their money and gold in return for safe passage.The fighters initially agreed and laid out a blanket, where Ms. Saleh placed her heart-shaped pendant and her gold rings, while the men left crumpled bills.

Instead of letting them go, the fighters began shoving the men outside, bound for death.

Sometime later, a fleet of cars arrived and the women, girls and children were driven away.

The Market

Months later, the Islamic State made clear in its online magazine that its campaign of enslaving Yazidi women and girls had been extensively preplanned.

"Prior to the taking of Sinjar, Shariah students in the Islamic State were tasked to research the Yazidis," said the English-language article, headlined "The Revival of Slavery Before the Hour," which appeared in the October issue of the magazine, Dabiq.

The article made clear that for the Yazidis, there was no chance to pay a tax known as jizya to be set free, "unlike the Jews and Christians."

"After capture, the Yazidi women and children were then divided according to the Shariah amongst the fighters of the Islamic State who participated in the Sinjar operations, after one fifth of the slaves were transferred to the Islamic State's authority to be divided" as spoils, the article said.

In much the same way as specific Bible passages were used centuries later to support the slave trade in the United States, the Islamic State cites specific verses or stories in the Quran or else in the Sunna, the traditions based on the sayings and deeds of the Prophet Muhammad, to justify their human trafficking, experts say.

Scholars of Islamic theology disagree, however, on the proper interpretation of these verses, and on the divisive question of whether Islam actually sanctions slavery.

Many argue that slavery figures in Islamic scripture in much the same way that it figures in the Bible — as a reflection of the period in antiquity in which the religion was born.

"In the milieu in which the Quran arose, there was a widespread practice of men having sexual relationships with unfree women," said Kecia Ali, an associate professor of religion at Boston University and the author of a book on slavery in early Islam. "It wasn't a particular religious institution. It was just how people did things."

Cole Bunzel, a scholar of Islamic theology at Princeton University, disagrees, pointing to the numerous references to the phrase "Those your right hand possesses" in the Quran, which for centuries has been interpreted to mean female slaves. He also points to the corpus of Islamic jurisprudence, which continues into the modern era and which he says includes detailed rules for the treatment of slaves.

"There is a great deal of scripture that sanctions slavery," said Mr. Bunzel, the author of a research paper published by the Brookings Institution on the ideology of the Islamic State.

"You can argue that it is no longer relevant and has fallen into abeyance. ISIS would argue that these institutions need to be revived, because that is what the Prophet and his companions did."

The youngest, prettiest women and girls were bought in the first weeks after their capture. Others — especially older, married women — described how they were transported from location to location, spending months in the equivalent of human holding pens, until a prospective buyer bid on them.

Their captors appeared to have a system in place, replete with its own methodology of inventorying the women, as well as their own lexicon. Women and girls were referred to as "Sabaya," followed by their name. Some were bought by wholesalers, who photographed and gave them numbers, to advertise them to potential buyers.

Osman Hassan Ali, a Yazidi businessman who has successfully smuggled out numerous Yazidi women, said he posed as a buyer in order to be sent the photographs. He shared a dozen images, each one showing a Yazidi woman sitting in a bare room on a couch, facing the camera with a blank, unsmiling expression. On the edge of the photograph is written in Arabic, "Sabaya No. 1," "Sabaya No. 2," and so on.

Buildings where the women were collected and held sometimes included a viewing room.

"When they put us in the building, they said we had arrived at the 'Sabaya Market,'" said one 19-year-old victim, whose first initial is I. "I understood we were now in a slave market."

She estimated there were at least 500 other unmarried women and girls in the multistory building, with the youngest among them being 11. When the buyers arrived, the girls were taken one by one into a separate room.

"The emirs sat against the wall and called us by name. We had to sit in a chair facing them. You had to look at them, and before you went in, they took away our scarves and anything we could have used to cover ourselves," she said.

"When it was my turn, they made me stand four times. They made me turn around."

The captives were also forced to answer intimate questions, including reporting the exact date of their last menstrual cycle. They realized that the fighters were trying to determine whether they were pregnant, in keeping with a Shariah rule stating that a man cannot have intercourse with his slave if she is pregnant.

Patrimony of ISIS

The use of sex slavery by the Islamic State initially surprised even the group's most ardent supporters, many of whom sparred with journalists online after the first reports of systematic rape.

The Islamic State's leadership has repeatedly sought to justify the practice to its internal audience.

After the initial article in Dabiq in October, the issue came up in the publication again this year, in an editorial in May that expressed the writer's hurt and dismay at the fact that some of the group's own sympathizers had questioned the institution of slavery. "What really alarmed me was that some of the Islamic State's supporters started denying the matter as if the soldiers of the Khilafah had committed a mistake or evil," the author wrote. "I write this while the letters drip of pride," she said. "We have indeed raided and captured the kafirah women and drove them like sheep by the edge of the sword." Kafirah refers to infidels.

A 25-year-old victim who escaped last month, identified by her first initial, A, described how one day her Libyan master handed her a laminated piece of paper. He explained that he had finished his training as a suicide bomber and was planning to blow himself up, and was therefore setting her free.

Labeled a "Certificate of Emancipation," the document was signed by the judge of the western province of the Islamic State. The Yazidi woman presented it at security checkpoints as she left Syria to return to Iraq, where she rejoined her family in July.

The Islamic State recently made it clear that sex with Christian and Jewish women captured in battle is also permissible, according to a new 34-page manual issued this summer by the terror group's Research and Fatwa Department.

Just about the only prohibition is having sex with a pregnant slave, and the manual describes how an owner must wait for a female captive to have her menstruating cycle, in order to "make sure there is nothing in her womb," before having intercourse with her. Of the 21 women and girls interviewed for this article, among the only ones who had not been raped were the women who were already pregnant at the moment of their capture, as well as those who were past menopause.

Beyond that, there appears to be no bounds to what is sexually permissible. Child rape is explicitly condoned: "It is permissible to have intercourse with the female slave who hasn't reached puberty, if she is fit for intercourse," according to a translation by the Middle East Media Research Institute of a pamphlet.

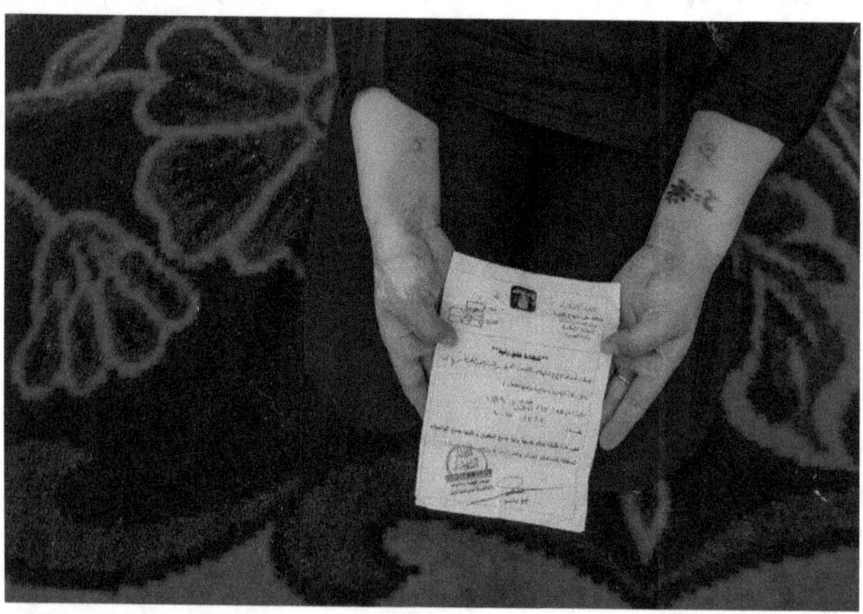

A 25-year-old Yazidi woman showed a "Certificate of Emancipation" given to her by a Libyan who had enslaved her. He explained that he had finished his training as a suicide bomber and was planning to blow himself up, and was therefore setting her free.

One 34-year-old Yazidi woman, who was bought and repeatedly raped by a Saudi fighter in the Syrian city of Shadadi, described how she fared better than the second slave in the household — a 12-year-old girl who was raped for days on end despite heavy bleeding.

"He destroyed her body. She was badly infected. The fighter kept coming and asking me, 'Why does she smell so bad?' And I said, she has an infection on the inside, you need to take care of her," the woman said.

Unmoved, he ignored the girl's agony, continuing the ritual of praying before and after raping the child.

"I said to him, 'She's just a little girl,' " the older woman recalled. "And he answered: 'No. She's not a little girl. She's a slave. And she knows exactly how to have sex.' "

"And having sex with her pleases God," he said.

The Terror Strategist

Secret Files Reveal the Structure of Islamic State

Aloof. Polite. Cajoling. Extremely attentive. Restrained. Dishonest. Inscrutable. Malicious.

The rebels from northern Syria, remembering encounters with him months later, recall completely different facets of the man. But they agree on one thing: "We never knew exactly who we were sitting across from."

In fact, not even those who shot and killed him after a brief firefight in the town of Tal Rifaat on a January morning in 2014 knew the true identity of the tall man in his late fifties. They were unaware that they had killed the strategic head of the group calling itself "Islamic State" (IS). The fact that this could have happened at all was the result of a rare but fatal miscalculation by the brilliant planner. The local rebels placed the body into a refrigerator, in which they intended to bury him. Only later, when they realized how important the man was, did they lift his body out again.

Samir Abd Muhammad al-Khlifawi was the real name of the Iraqi, whose bony features were softened by a white beard. But no one knew him by that name. Even his best-known pseudonym, Haji Bakr, wasn't widely known. But that was precisely part of the plan. The former colonel in the intelligence service of Saddam Hussein's air defense force had been secretly pulling the strings at IS for years. Former members of the group had repeatedly mentioned him as one of its leading figures. Still, it was never clear what exactly his role was.

But when the architect of the Islamic State died, he left something behind that he had intended to keep strictly confidential: the blueprint for this state. It is a folder full of handwritten organizational charts, lists and schedules, which describe how a country can be gradually subjugated. SPIEGEL has gained exclusive access to the 31 pages, some consisting of several pages pasted together. They reveal a multilayered composition and directives for action, some already tested and others newly devised for the anarchical situation in Syria's rebel-held territories. In a sense, the documents are the source code of the most successful terrorist army in recent history.

Until now, much of the information about IS has come from fighters who had defected and data sets from the IS internal administration seized in Baghdad. But none of this offered an explanation for the group's meteoric rise to prominence, before air strikes in the late summer of 2014 put a stop to its triumphal march.

For the first time, the Haji Bakr documents now make it possible to reach conclusions on how the IS leadership is organized and what role former officials in the government of ex-dictator Saddam Hussein play in it. Above all, however, they show how the takeover in northern Syria was planned, making the group's later advances into Iraq possible in the first place. In addition, months of research undertaken by SPIEGEL in Syria, as well as other newly discovered records, exclusive to SPIEGEL, show that Haji Bakr's instructions were carried out meticulously.

Bakr's documents were long hidden in a tiny addition to a house in embattled northern Syria. Reports of their existence were first made by an eyewitness who had seen them in Haji Bakr's house shortly after his death. In April 2014, a single page from the file was smuggled to Turkey, where SPIEGEL was able to examine it for the first time. It only became possible to reach Tal Rifaat to evaluate the entire set of handwritten papers in November 2014.

What ISIS Really Wants

The Islamic State is no mere collection of psychopaths. It is a religious group with carefully considered beliefs, among them that it is a key agent of the coming apocalypse. Here's what that means for its strategy—and for how to stop it.

Where did it come from, and what are its intentions? The simplicity of these questions can be deceiving, and few Western leaders seem to know the answers. In December, The New York Times published confidential comments by Major General Michael K. Nagata, the Special Operations commander for the United States in the Middle East, admitting that he had hardly begun figuring out the Islamic State's appeal. "We have not defeated the idea," he said. "We do not even understand the idea." In the past year, President Obama has referred to the Islamic State, variously, as "not

Islamic" and as al-Qaeda's "jayvee team," statements that reflected confusion about the group, and may have contributed to significant strategic errors.

The group seized Mosul, Iraq, last June, and already rules an area larger than the United Kingdom. Abu Bakr al-Baghdadi has been its leader since May 2010, but until last summer, his most recent known appearance on film was a grainy mug shot from a stay in U.S. captivity at Camp Bucca during the occupation of Iraq. Then, on July 5 of last year, he stepped into the pulpit of the Great Mosque of al-Nuri in Mosul, to deliver a Ramadan sermon as the first caliph in generations—upgrading his resolution from grainy to high-definition, and his position from hunted guerrilla to commander of all Muslims. The inflow of jihadists that followed, from around the world, was unprecedented in its pace and volume, and is continuing.

Our ignorance of the Islamic State is in some ways understandable: It is a hermit kingdom; few have gone there and returned. Baghdadi has spoken on camera only once. But his address, and the Islamic State's countless other propaganda videos and encyclicals, are online, and the caliphate's supporters have toiled mightily to make their project knowable. We can gather that their state rejects peace as a matter of principle; that it hungers for genocide; that its religious views make it constitutionally incapable of certain types of change, even if that change might ensure its survival; and that it considers itself a harbinger of—and headline player in—the imminent end of the world.

The Problem with Vows to 'Defeat' the Islamic State

What happens after Raqqa falls?

ISIS has suffered territorial losses on multiple fronts, including in Iraq, Libya, and Syria. The organization may look nearer to defeat than at any time in the past two years, but there is still a great deal of fighting to be done before the group is destroyed, or more likely beaten back to an underground terrorist organization as it was in 2009. In a previous post, we argued that truly defeating the ISIS threat would be more expensive than most now recognize, and beyond what most Americans would be willing to pay, leaving containment as the only viable option. Ambassador James Jeffrey disagrees.

In particular, he argues that the United States and its allies should reinforce today's U.S. force of roughly 5,000 soldiers with another 10,000 troops, order them to lead a conventional ground offensive against ISIS, and loosen the rules of engagement for ground fighting and air strikes to tolerate more civilian casualties. With these policies, Jeffrey argues, ISIS can be defeated promptly. Once Raqqa falls, the real U.S. mission is complete in his view. He doesn't say what those 15,000 soldiers should do then, but he's opposed to a costly stabilization mission and implies that U.S. troops should instead go home and avoid further commitment.

We agree that stabilization is too expensive. But we disagree with Jeffrey on the merits of a smash-and-leave conventional offensive. In our view, such a policy actually secures none of the interests that nominally motivate it.

Jeffrey's argument is a variation on a theme that is increasingly prominent among analysts frustrated with the long U.S. counterinsurgencies in Afghanistan and Iraq: The United States should adopt a policy of waging decisive conventional warfare against states without worrying overmuch about what happens afterwards when the target regime is toppled. But this position isn't actually new—it represents a return to the de facto.

Leave Root Causes Aside—Destroy the ISIS 'State'

Of course it would be daunting to solve the conflicts the Islamic State feeds on. But that isn't, or shouldn't be, the mission.

America Can't Do Much About ISIS, advocated containing the Islamic State and questioned America's ability to destroy the group. The first problem with this analysis is how the authors define "destroy ISIS." They compare the amorphous fight against al-Qaeda with the one against ISIS, discussing how to get at the roots of its terrorist ideology and fix the ungoverned space that provides its sanctuary. This leads them repeatedly to conflate destroying ISIS in its current form as a quasi-state with the monumental task of resolving the Syrian Civil War and the Sunni-Shia split in Iraq. To the contrary, if the mission is properly defined, America can destroy ISIS, and must.

Defeating ISIS-as-state is not dependent upon solving Syria as a social, historical, cultural, religious, and governance project, let alone doing the same with Iraq. ISIS feeds on the conflicts in both countries and makes the situation in both worse. But it is possible to defeat ISIS as a "state" and as a military-economic "power"—that is, deal with the truly threatening part— without having to solve the Syrian and Iraqi crises or eliminate ISIS as a set of terrorist cells or source of ideological inspiration. Of course, even if ISIS is destroyed as a state, we would still have the Syrian Civil War and Iraqi disunity, but we have all that now, along with ISIS, which presents its own challenges to the region and the West.

Normally, if one opts not to ignore a foreign-policy problem, the two choices are: Fix it (which in ISIS's case would mean defeat and destroy it, per America's official policy), or contain it. The choice is made based on an analysis of the likely costs and risks of eliminating the problem versus those of living with it, as well as the impact of one's decision on broader concerns. From both points of view, Biddle and Shapiro's arguments are flawed.

Admittedly the costs of destroying ISIS as a jihadist ideological movement, and its remnants as an insurgency (i.e., what it was in Iraq before 2014), not to speak of "fixing" Syria and Iraq, are just as daunting as Biddle and Shapiro repeatedly argue. But that isn't, or shouldn't be, the mission. The mission should be crushing ISIS as a state and as a military and economic power. That is a different challenge, and one far more responsive to conventional military power. Local forces with minimal U.S. indirect support have already made progress in some areas, including recently in Shadadi, Syria, and Ramadi, Iraq. ISIS has fewer foot soldiers than at any time since 2014, and has problems, as the authors note, paying its bills.

A much more robust indirect support package of advisers, artillery, and attack helicopters, more special-operations raids, and even more liberal rules of engagement for air strikes than those just adopted (decentralizing strike decisions, accepting slightly higher risk of civilian casualties, and using more airpower and more powerful bombs) could generate more rapid victories. A limited commitment of U.S. ground troops—two brigades of 5,000 troops each, reinforced by other NATO forces, along with local allies—could make even more rapid progress. These would supplement the 5,000 or so American troops now in Iraq training local forces and the 250 special-operations forces just deployed to Syria. Thus even a tweaking of current U.S. indirect support (now in the works), and certainly limited direct American combat, could destroy ISIS relatively rapidly as a "state" and "army." That would leave a "day after" problem, but would solve ISIS-as-a-state. And the U.S., at least sometimes, has effectively dealt with such "days after" without massive American troop presence, from northern Iraq after the Gulf War in 1991, to Kosovo, El Salvador, and Colombia. But even a messy post-ISIS situation is better than containment, given that course's dangers and costs. It's those, which the authors largely ignore, that have to be weighed against the costs of destroying the ISIS state. The best place to build credibility, with maximum chance of success and least escalation risk, is the fight against ISIS.

Right now, maintaining troops and dealing with millions of internally displaced persons is bankrupting the Iraqi state (and the Kurdistan government) and generating much political turbulence. If those governments start collapsing, any "containment" strategy would as well.

The Syrian Civil War, unchecked, eventually spawned ISIS, a migration crisis straining Europe, and a worrisome Russian intervention.

Until ISIS is destroyed as a state, it can still launch horrific terrorist attacks, provoke political collapse in Baghdad or among the Iraqi Kurds, and even trigger a descent into a Sunni-Shia regional conflict, if Shia Iran targets ISIS and thereby threatens the Sunni Arab territory in which ISIS is nested. (ISIS remnants could still threaten terrorist attacks, but not of the same magnitude or with the same geostrategic consequences.)

The second consideration in any decision about how to handle a foreign-policy problem is its impact on broader foreign relations. For example, in 2007, the U.S. opted not to act itself against Syria's secret al-Kibar nuclear reactor, which Israel destroyed in an airstrike that year. This was not because U.S. action was less risky than an Israeli attack, but largely because America's "plate" in the Middle East was full with two wars, along with negotiations over Iran's nuclear program and the Israeli-Palestinian conflict. But today, after Obama's 2013 failure to enforce his self-declared "red line" against the use of chemical weapons in Syria by the forces of Syrian president Bashar al-Assad, the U.S. needs to build credibility that it will follow up threats of force with action to counter states like Iran, Russia, China, and North Korea that threaten the existing global order. The best place to build such credibility, with maximum chance of success and least escalation risk, is the fight against ISIS.

Finally, Biddle and Shapiro's arguments all would have sounded equally reasonable if made against Russian President Vladimir Putin's Syrian intervention. But he went ahead, and with a fraction of America's diplomatic and military capabilities achieved a limited but important victory, avoiding the "quagmire" President Obama predicted. And America can't?

America Can't Do Much About ISIS

That leaves patience, containment, and humanitarian aid as the least-bad policies while waiting for this awful war to play itself out.

In 2003, David Petraeus, then a division commander in Iraq, famously asked "tell me how this ends?" in reference to the conflict just starting there. It was a good question then, and it's a good question now. The war against the Islamic State gets a lot of attention, much of it focused on the immediate: Is the war going better or worse this month than last month? Is the Islamic State gaining ground or losing it? Are U.S. air strikes killing more Islamic State leaders or fewer? But these things only matter if they contribute to an ultimate end to the conflict on terms the United States can live with. Will they?

In fact, we have a lot of evidence on wars like this and how they typically end. But it's not a very encouraging story. The Islamic State threat is likely to persist, in one form or another, for a long time. In the meantime, we're going to be stuck with a policy that amounts to containment and damage limitation, whose shortcomings will frustrate many Americans.

Civil wars of the kind in which the U.S. conflict with the Islamic State is embedded are notoriously hard to terminate and typically drag on for years. Datasets vary slightly, but most put the median duration of such conflicts at seven to 10 years; and an important minority drag on for a generation or more.

When they do end, it's rarely because an empowered, victorious army marches into the enemy capital, pulls down the flag, and governs a newly stable society. Civil wars like today's conflict in Syria and Iraq are often complex, multi-sided proxy conflicts in which a variety of local combatants have ties to outside backers who fund, equip, train, and advise allies' forces. This outside support enables fighters to weather setbacks and hang on in the face of military adversity. Outside backers usually have geopolitical reasons of their own to support local proxies, and for most such backers, a stable postwar state under rivals' influence often looks worse than continued chaos—so outsiders also usually have incentives to keep the pot boiling by supporting guerrilla resistance if their proxies lose outright control of territory. But with outside backers on all sides injecting money and arms as needed to prevent a stable consolidation of power by rivals, the result can be a long, grinding stalemate wherein no one can establish durable control over a stabilized country. Instead, it's often mutual exhaustion that finally ends such wars. War burns capital and destroys wealth. Even the most resilient combatants eventually run their war-supporting economies so far into the ground that they simply cannot continue. And even their outside backers eventually burn through enough of their own wealth that they lose enthusiasm for the project. When this happens, bargaining space for negotiated settlements opens up, and peace talks can finally end the fighting. The civil war in Angola following the country's independence, for example, lasted 19 years and only ended in 1994, following the cessation of external support and the exhaustion of both rebel and government forces.

Sadly, fighting resumed in 1998, but without external support for the combatants, it was short-lived; a durable settlement appears to have been reached in 2002, following almost 30 years of intermittent fighting.

Real exhaustion of this kind could take a long time in Syria and Iraq, and leave a lot of profound damage in its wake. To date, Iran, Russia, Saudi Arabia, the United Arab Emirates, and of course the United States, among others, have all supported proxies in Syria and Iraq. This list includes countries with some very deep pockets. Iran and Saudi Arabia, in particular, each see the war in Syria and Iraq as essential to prevent the other from seizing a geopolitical advantage in a regional conflict for survival. Russia has been willing to deploy its own troops to prevent its ally, Syrian President Bashar al-Assad, from falling. Local allies of all these parties have suffered reversals but have often been bailed out, given the stakes their backers see in the war; for any major combatant to be defeated will thus require a degree of war-weariness not yet apparent from any of the major outside benefactors.

What, then, of the U.S. war against the Islamic State? ISIS is more self-reliant than many contestants in this conflict, funding its war effort mainly by taxing economic activity in areas it controls. The Islamic State lacks the kind of outside benefactors that fuel Assad's or Jabhat al-Nusra's or the Iraqi government's war efforts. And as the group's ongoing incompetent governance destroys the economy in areas it controls, ISIS will likely run out of money sooner than many of the war's other combatants. Indeed, it may already be showing signs of this: In late November 2015, the group slashed its fighters' salaries in half, reporting in Western media suggests its revenues have plummeted, and the group has reportedly tried to create cash through exchange-rate manipulations (a doomed strategy for small economies, as former finance ministers from Mexico, Thailand, Argentina, and other developing economies could attest).

The real problem, however, runs much deeper than just the Islamic State. The war in Iraq and Syria pits a host of groups against one another, many of whom are almost as dangerous to U.S. interests as the Islamic State, and many of whom seek the same status of jihadi vanguard against the West that ISIS now enjoys. ISIS itself achieved this position at the expense of the al-Qaeda-affiliated Jabhat al-Nusra, with whom it competes actively for recruits and resources. Even if some U.S.-allied proxy succeeds in conquering the nominal Islamic State capital of Raqqa and pulling down the ISIS flag from its citadel, this is unlikely to end the war, stabilize Syria, or even remove the threat of jihadi terrorism against the United States from Syrian (or Iraqi) soil—it would just open the war to its next phase, in which Islamic State's rivals compete for the status that group had enjoyed before them. In the absence of a mutual willingness to end the war and accept some new model of representative governance, even great progress against ISIS does not realize U.S. interests in the conflict—which are to end the terrorism threat, the humanitarian crisis, and the danger to regional stability, not merely to occupy the city of Raqqa. A mutual willingness to end the war on the part of most or all of today's warring factions, however, seems a long way off. U.S. leverage to bring about a real end to the war—and actual realization of American interests in that war—is distinctly limited. None of the proposals popular in today's Washington debate offer any meaningful prospect of achieving this. According to U.S. military doctrine, to defeat even an insurgency (much less a proto-state like ISIS) and stabilize a threatened population requires something like 20 counterinsurgents for every thousand civilians. That means 50,000-100,000 well-trained troops would be needed to hold the area now under Islamic State control (depending on how much of the population has fled), much less the rest of Syria. No one is now proposing a realistic plan to accomplish anything close to this—whether such a force comprises American troops, Iraqis, Kurds, Saudis, Turks, or anyone else. In the absence of this, bombing raids or offensives from Iraqi or Kurdish allies can accelerate the rate at which ISIS burns through its capital and perhaps hasten the day when the Islamic State is replaced by the next militant group in the queue—but limited efforts of this kind cannot end the war.

The most important contribution Americans can make in Syria and Iraq might not be on the battlefield at all. If this war plays out the way so many others have, its end will come not through an allied offensive to conquer a capital city but through the mutual exhaustion of multiple actors with multiple, often wealthy outside benefactors. This will eventually happen—but it will likely take many years yet. U.S. efforts won't change these fundamentals much absent a major stabilization and nation-building effort that few Americans now support, or some diplomatic breakthrough that assuages Iranian, Russian, and Saudi long-run security concerns. And that leaves Americans with patience and containment as the least-bad policy while waiting for this awful war to play itself out.

If that's the case, the most important contribution Americans can make in Syria and Iraq might well not be on the battlefield at all. A smart containment strategy should include serious efforts to assist regional powers in coping with the humanitarian fallout of Syrian and Iraqi violence, to limit the risk that neighboring states suffer those countries' fate, and to encourage long-run political settlements where possible. Providing support to Iraq, Jordan, and Turkey to help them provide reasonable conditions for refugees so their skills do not atrophy and their children are educated must be part of any successful policy. So too must be active diplomatic engagement with the Iraqi government to ensure it provides reasonable governance to its Sunni population, something it did not do for three years prior to the Islamic State's military successes in Iraq in 2014. (Indeed, recent polling shows that while the vast majority of Sunnis across Iraq oppose the Islamic State, those in ISIS-occupied Mosul do not want to be "liberated" by the Iraqi Army, likely because they fear and distrust state security forces as well as Kurdish and Shiite paramilitaries.)

And humanitarian assistance might also help reduce the terrorism threat in the West. The best intelligence system for detecting plots like the ones that have so recently traumatized Brussels, Istanbul, and Paris is the active cooperation of the populations within which the terrorists seek to hide. The greater the misery among dispossessed, poorly housed, poorly fed populations, the greater the anger that can fuel terrorism and the less prone such populations and expatriate communities in the West will be to assist Western counterterrorism efforts. Humanitarian aid is not just an appropriate response to suffering—given the limits on what available military options can accomplish, aid may be one of our most important counter-terrorism tools, too.

Why ISIS Propaganda Works

As it stands, the international coalition is far from winning the information war against the Islamic State. Its air strikes may be squeezing the group in Iraq and Syria and killing many of its leaders, but that has not halted the self-proclaimed caliphate's ideological momentum. Indeed, at the end of 2015, it was estimated that the number of foreigners travelling to join militant groups in Iraq and Syria—predominantly the Islamic State—had more than doubled in the course of just 18 months. What's more, while these figures may be striking, sheer numbers are less important than intent when it comes to the organization's actual threat to the world. As we have already seen, it takes a very small number of people to unleash great terror, whether in Iraq, Syria, or elsewhere.

Abu Bakr al-Baghdadi's organization does not enjoy mass appeal, but it is certainly having mass impact. After but 18 months of caliphate-hood, the group's preeminence is already coming to shape what it is to be a millennial Muslim and inspiring attacks far outside the caliphate. Hence, the strategic communications war—where hearts and minds are won and lost—is just as important in the long-term as any military campaign, if not more so. To be fair to the coalition, it has not missed the ideational menace that the Islamic State presents. As a direct result of coalition efforts, especially those of the United States government, counter-Islamic State information operations are more prolific now than ever before, the quantity of counterpropaganda is snowballing, and social-media giants like Twitter are being more aggressive in their efforts to hobble ISIS propagandists. Even Anonymous has thrown its hat in the ring.

The coalition's information operations are facing an almost insurmountable challenge. Such a state of affairs is untenable. To ameliorate it, a new communications architecture is required, based on three pillars: global strategic direction, local delivery, and a broader, more accurate understanding of how and why the Islamic State appeals. It's no secret that the caliphate has a compelling story, coupled with a sophisticated ability to deliver it. But what is often overlooked are the underlying strategic elements that enable the group to land its messages so effectively.

First, while the international media tends to obsess over the Islamic State's ultraviolence, the group's propaganda is incredibly varied. Unlike the coalition's primary weapon in the information war—negative messaging—the caliphal narrative combines positive and negative themes that appeal to both ideological and political supporters. On a daily basis, the group parades images of civilian life, ruminates upon the concept of mercy, and highlights the visceral camaraderie allegedly felt among its members. Crucially, it doesn't just do this online—propaganda is just as important in person in the Islamic State's heartlands as it is on its members' smartphones.

The Islamic State expends huge amounts of energy building this composite narrative because its propaganda is being created for, and directed to, a number of audiences: potential members, sympathizers, enemies, general publics—the list goes on. Whoever they are, the Islamic State propagandists tie them all together by communicating the same core narrative to each—that its caliphate is a triumphant, model society that offers community to all who desire it, and destruction to those who don't.

To active supporters and potential sympathizers, in particular, the power of this narrative steamrolls the coalition's counter-messaging, which is currently set up only to address a handful of discrete strands of the Islamic State idea, instead of the core narrative in its entirety. This has led, at times, to coalition counter-messaging being bogged down by well-intentioned but questionable reproductions of the Islamic State's ultra violence, and social-media posts intoning variations on "The Islamic State is brutal and isn't Islamic so don't join it."

The Islamic State's media team evidently recognizes that in the digital-communications age, everyone—from sympathizers to adversaries—can be a tactical instrument of propaganda. Reflecting this, they have made the strategic choice to not pigeonhole themselves by reaching out just to sworn believers in jihadism or those that they consider to be potential supporters, as coalition governments so often do in their counter-messaging efforts.

By catering to a wider set of audiences, ISIS propagandists reinforce their message gradually to build layered support, which is made all the more sustainable because they retain astonishingly tight command of the Islamic State brand. Indeed, despite its geographic spread, the caliphate's dispersed network of 48 official media offices—one for each self-declared "province" (of which it claims 19 in Syria and Iraq, 7 in Yemen, 3 in Libya, and various others corresponding to its footholds in additional countries) and nine additional, centrally administered outlets—seemingly never goes off message, always transmitting the same carefully constructed ideas of the triumphant, defiant caliphate and the promise of community. As recent video sets regarding the Saudi Arabia-led Islamic alliance against terrorism, the Paris attacks, and the refugee crisis demonstrate, if the "Base Foundation"—which is how the Islamic State refers to its "corporate headquarters"—issues a communique saying "Jump," all its provincial foundations are on standby to say "How high?" and respond a few days later with the on-message HD fruits of their labor.

Critically, the aggregate impact of the offices is greatly amplified because, instead of disseminating the material themselves, the ISIS outreach team actively cultivates unofficial spokespeople who share their media outside the caliphate's formal communications structure, encouraging others around the world to autonomously spread the Islamic State message alongside them. Because those unofficial propagandists are best-suited to identifying the ideal channel for reaching their respective local audiences—and tailoring the core narrative accordingly the influence of the Islamic State's communications skyrockets. For the coalition to have lasting communications impact against this formidable enemy, it requires a similarly nuanced—and expansive—understanding of message delivery and audience segmentation. Twitter suspensions are not nearly enough.

As it stands, the coalition's counter-messaging is not structured to attack the Islamic State's entire narrative, but instead looks at and attacks specific elements of its messages individually. This structural weakness is compounded by a lack of credible voices and a surplus of risk-averseness, in large part because these efforts have, so far at least, been both led and delivered by a handful of Western governments. The resulting, overly bureaucratic approach persistently gets in the way of flexibility and dynamism, both of which are required for success.

Government-directed initiatives are fighting an unwinnable battle. They are too centralized, too rigorously managed, and too reactive. It's an uncomfortable truth that, no matter how well-intentioned they are, governments' ideational responses to jihadism have been marked by memorable slip-ups and controversies. The media is always quick to report on things done wrong, and tends to steer clear of assessing successes.

As such, no matter how much rebranding and restructuring takes place, efforts like the U.S.'s "Shared Values" campaign (an early-2000s set of commercials aiming to show Muslims living happy lives in the U.S., which was mocked as the "Happy Muslim" campaign); the ultraviolent approach to counterpropaganda embodied in a State Department's "Think Again Turn Away" campaign (which, in purporting to show "some truths about terrorism," disseminated gory videos among other things); and government officials swapping insults with jihadists on Twitter tend to be the most memorable, defining points for U.S. forays into counter-jihadist public diplomacy. And, while it's true that for every mistake there is a success story, even those are but drops in the information ocean. Indeed, even when supplemented by the efforts of the newly formed £10 million UK-based Coalition Communications Cell—not to mention other strategic-communications centers proliferating globally, from Nigeria to Malaysia—overtly government-directed initiatives are fighting an unwinnable battle. They are too centralized, too rigorously managed, and too reactive. The amount of their activity is structurally bound to be insufficient, and its content bound to lack credibility among the most at-risk target audiences.

Marginalized communities that feel indifferent or hostile to their respective governments, let alone supporters and potential sympathizers of Mr. al-Baghdadi, will never, ever be swayed by a foreign state telling them on social media that the Islamic State's caliphate is not Islamic or that it is killing more Muslims than anyone else. For that reason, even initiatives that are ostensibly tailored to be more "local," like the UAE's Sawab Center ("the first-ever multinational online messaging and engagement program," which operates in overt partnership with the U.S. government), are bound to struggle, simply for the fact that their messaging is unable to truly resonate with the right people.

To be sure, the people that matter have not missed this problem. In June 2015, for example, Rashad Hussain, former coordinator of the U.S. Center for Strategic Counterterrorism Communications, noted that Islamic State recruits and sympathizers are "almost always influenced by a figure in their community who uses grievance and ideology to reel them in." Such recognition is all well and good, but there is a big difference between not missing a problem and being able to take effective action to mitigate it. What needs to happen is, in conceptual terms, simple. Instead of governments, the burden for reaching potential Islamic State supporters must rest entirely on the shoulders of local, non-government actors. They can be Muslim or non-Muslim, individuals or institutions, community leaders or cultural organizations. What matters most is that they are trusted as enemies of the Islamic State and hold preexisting and offline relationships with—and are respected by—those at risk of radicalization, the communities around those at risk of radicalization, and the general audience being targeted by the Islamic State's propagandists. It is crucial that they are not perceived as being under the thumb of the coalition's Western leadership.

To achieve this separation, governments should provide funding, logistical support, and training in communications best practices, whether to groups already doing counter-radicalization work or to those wishing to start from scratch. Since all this must contribute toward the shared goal of undermining the Islamic State's brand, it will only work if governments never publicly endorse these actors or include their communications on official channels, unless specifically requested otherwise. With governmental support and the coalition's core messaging priorities in hand, local actors will be able to benefit from a globally coordinated campaign that will, in theory, amplify the anti-Islamic State message more widely, in turn creating a better condition for success in each local context. There are two major benefits to empowering such communicators. First, doing so would dramatically increase the volume of audience engagements, which is a fast way to expand the number of people delivering anti-Islamic State communications. Second, and more importantly, using the right channel to broadcast to each audience increases a message's impact.

Local actors are incomparably better-placed to identify the best channel for communicating than distant governments. Governments still have an integral role to play in the communications battle with the Islamic State. But they must shift their primary information activities away from direct communications, to flexibly supporting and trusting local actors to deliver messages on their behalf—a model reminiscent of that currently employed by the Islamic State.

Syrian Civil War detailed map

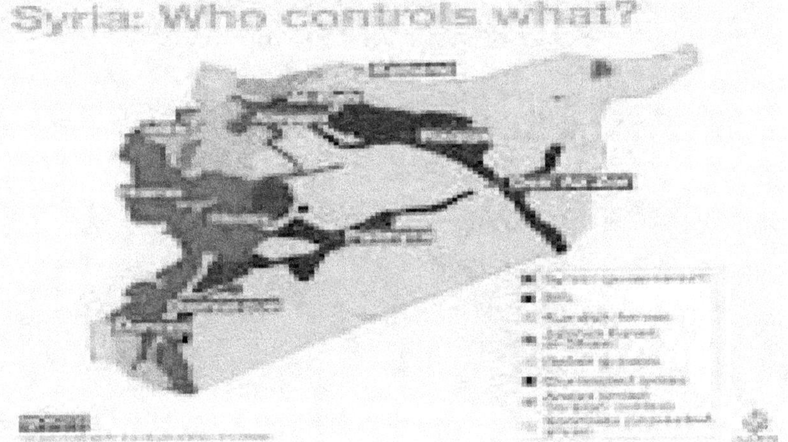

Syria: Who controls what?

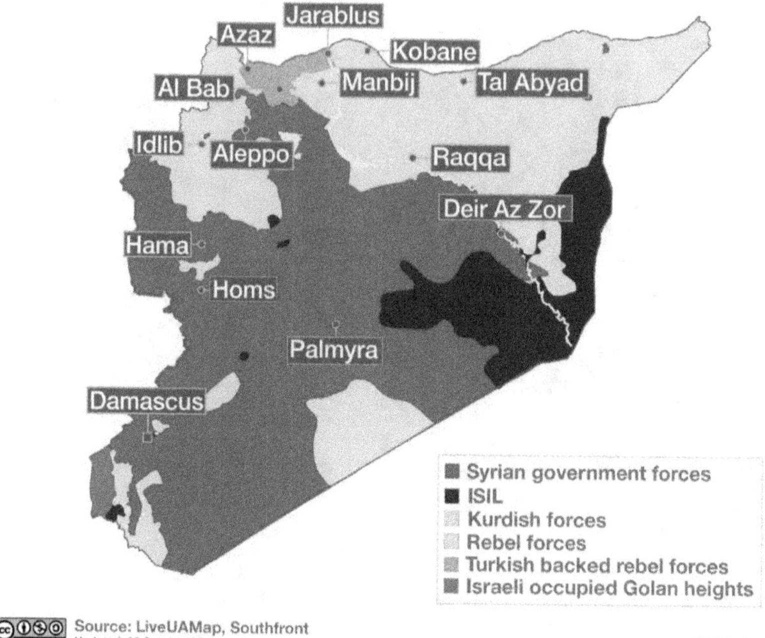

Source: LiveUAMap, Southfront
Updated: 29 October 2017

@AJLabs ALJAZEERA

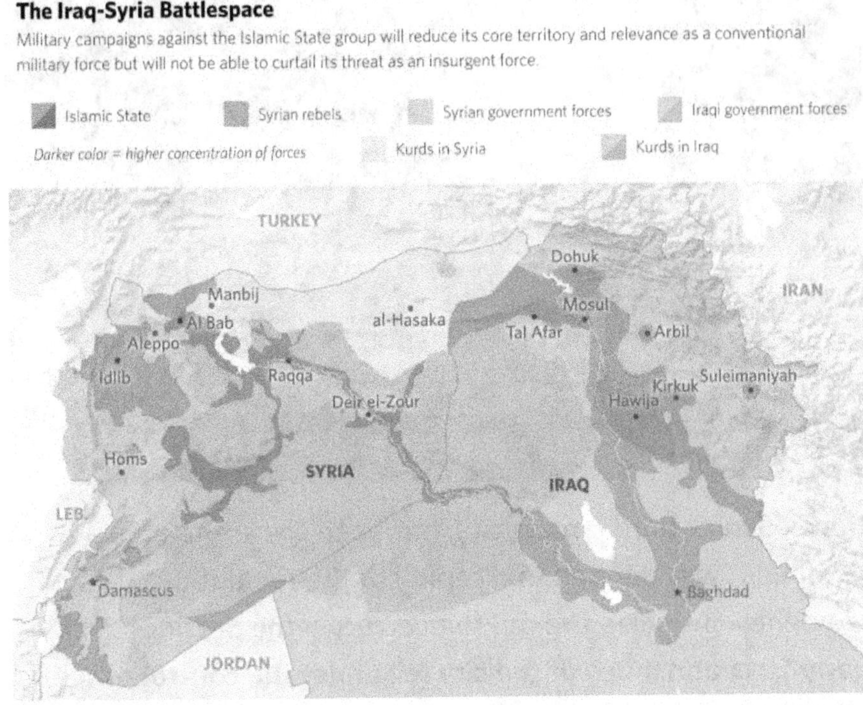

Syria: Mapping the conflict

Territorial control in Syria has changed many times since the country's uprising began more than four years ago, with long periods of attrition characterising the conflict.

However, there are now signs the battlefield is transforming, with extremist and Islamist groups establishing a momentum of their own and the forces of Syrian president, Bashar al-Assad, under mounting pressure on severalsl fronts.

Homs, Syria's third largest city, has been the scene of heavy fighting. It was dubbed the 'capital of the revolution' after residents embraced the call to overthrow the president in early 2011 and much of the city fell under the control of the opposition. However, government forces gradually took back areas held by rebels and in May 2014, the city was fully regained by regime troops. Fighting continues to the east of the city between the government, IS and other opposition forces.

The Syrian capital and its outskirts remain a key strategic area of control. While the regime has succeeded in using sieges and intensive air strike campaigns to negotiate truces with various armed groups in and around the city, fighting continues between government forces and opposition fighters. Government forces have reportedly begun fortifying approaches to Damascus and Latakia in the north west in order to protect their core territory.

Fighting broke out in Syria's largest city in July 2012 with rebels taking control of a number of districts. However their offensive stalled and the battle became a war of attrition. The city continues to be a key battleground between Syrian government forces, rebels and jihadists. Fighting and government air strikes have left thousands dead, and destroyed more than 60% of the Old City, a Unesco World Heritage site.

Syrian rebels have made gains in the southern cities of Deraa and Quneitra, where groups have remained relatively united. In June, they seized the Syrian government's largest military base in Deraa, though this is far from the rebels' stated goal of reaching rural Damascus.

To the north, Kurdish forces have been battling a series of deadly IS counter-attacks. The jihadist group had, until then, suffered a series of defeats in areas along the Turkish border since being forced to withdraw from the town of Kobane in January.

Most recently, the Kurdish Popular Protection Units (YPG) - supported by rebels and US-led coalition airstrikes - recaptured the border town of Tal Abyad, to the east of Kobane, in June.

For the Syrian government, battling this fractured opposition has taken its toll, according to the ISW. The regime is facing a manpower shortage and has attempted to counteract it with conscription campaigns and an increased use of Iranian-sponsored paramilitary forces, it says.

Over the coming months, the ISW predicts that jihadist groups, such as IS and al-Nusra Front, will gain in influence and power, while Iran - the Syrian government's strategic ally - and Saudi Arabia - a backer of rebel forces - will escalate their involvement in Syria.

The conflict has its roots in protests that erupted in Deraa city in March 2011 after the arrest and torture of some teenagers who painted revolutionary slogans on a school wall.

Opposition supporters - angered by the government's use of lethal force to crush pro-democracy demonstrations - first began to take up arms to defend themselves and later to expel security forces from their local areas.

As the country descended into civil war, armed rebel brigades battled government forces for control of cities, towns and swathes of countryside. During 2012, rebel forces enjoyed a series of tactical successes, taking control of several outlying suburbs and towns around Damascus, and ousting troops from large parts of the second city of Aleppo.

However, the advances were not decisive. By the start of 2013, the government began to recapture opposition strongholds around the capital, while there was stalemate in Aleppo, with the city divided into rebel and loyalist-controlled sectors.

Then, in June 2013, government troops backed by fighters from the Lebanese Shia Islamist movement, Hezbollah, recaptured a number of rebel strongholds.

Rebel forces have been affected by deep divisions among groups. Secular moderates are now outnumbered by Islamists and jihadists linked to al-Qaeda, whose brutal tactics have caused widespread concern and triggered rebel infighting.

Humanitarian crisis

The escalating violence and IS advances have had a significant humanitarian impact on Syria and its neighbours.

Syria is now the world's biggest internal displacement crisis, with more than seven million people forced from their homes but remaining in the country.

Meanwhile, more than 4 million people have fled the country's borders, mainly taking refuge in surrounding countries.

Turkey and Lebanon have each taken in more than one million Syrians, while Jordan, Iraq and Egypt have become home to hundreds of thousands more.

The battle for Raqqa

An intensive aerial bombardment by the US-led coalition helped secure victory in Raqqa for the Syrian Democratic Forces (SDF), which was formed in 2015 by the the Kurdish Popular Protection Units (YPG) militia and a number of smaller, Arab factions. Since early June, coalition planes have carried out almost 4,000 air strikes on the city.

Estimates of the number of casualties vary. The Syrian Observatory for Human Rights, a UK-based monitoring group, said at least 3,250 people had been killed, among them 1,130 civilians. Other groups say the total was higher.

The UN estimates about 270,000 people fled their homes during the SDF offensive.

The immense task of rebuilding the city may take years. Clearing operations are already under way to uncover any jihadist sleeper cells and remove landmines.

The jihadists exploited the chaos and divisions within both Syria and Iraq.

IS grew out of what was al-Qaeda in Iraq, which was formed by Sunni militants after the US-led invasion in 2003 and became a major force in the country's sectarian insurgency.

In 2011, the group joined the rebellion against President Bashar al-Assad in Syria, where it found a safe haven and easy access to weapons.

At the same time, it took advantage of the withdrawal of US troops from Iraq, as well as widespread Sunni anger at the sectarian policies of the country's Shia-led government.

In 2013, the group began seizing control of territory in Syria and changed its name to Islamic State in Iraq and the Levant (Isis or Isil).Isis overran large swathes of northern and western Iraq, proclaimed the creation of a "caliphate", and became known as "Islamic State".

A subsequent advance into areas controlled by Iraq's Kurdish minority, and the killing or enslaving of thousands of members of the Yazidi religious group, prompted the US-led coalition to begin air strikes on IS positions in Iraq in August 2014.

As IS is now being forced out of Iraq and Syria, another problem is the likely resurgence of hostilities between rival groups. Already Iraqi forces have pushed the Kurds back from land they took during the fight against IS around Kirkuk. More than five million Syrians have fled abroad to escape the fighting in Syria, according to the UN. Most have ended up in neighboring Turkey, Lebanon and Jordan.

About 970,000 Syrians applied for asylum in Europe between April 2011 and July 2017, according to UN figures.

The UN estimates there are more than three million Iraqis who have been forced to leave their homes to escape the conflict with IS and are displaced within the country.

The battle for control of Mosul led to about one million people fleeing their homes - about 800,000 are still living in temporary camps or with relatives.

A journey into Raqqa, the heart of Isis's failed caliphate

Raqqa lies in ruins, the last Isis fighters bussed out in an evacuation deal to regroup in the desert. Our reporter found a city that may never recover and a war that is far from over

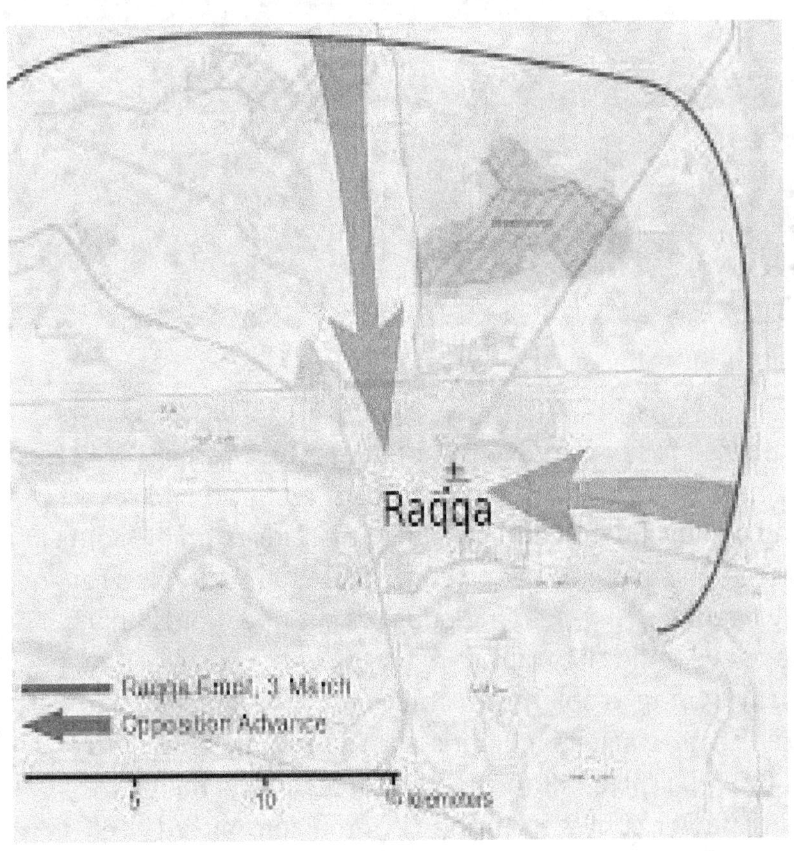

The expected fall of

Success will bring problems for the victors as well as the defeated. The attackers in Ra

The expected fall of Raqqa will mark the latest defeat for ISIS as it loses its last urban strongholds in Syria and Iraq and reverts to being a guerrilla movement launching raids from hideouts in the desert. The siege of Raqqa started on 6 June and Isis fought skilfully against overwhelming odds until it now holds only a small enclave amid the ruins.

Success will bring problems for the victors as well as the defeated. The attackers in Raqqa are the Syrian Democratic Forces (SDF) , a mixed Kurdish-Arab force, but its military punching power comes from the YPG, the committed, well-organized and experienced Syrian Kurdish fighters linked to Kurdistan Workers Party (PKK) in Turkey. The SDF have shown that they are excellent ground troops, but they owe their sweeping successes not only to their undoubted military prowess but also the devastating firepower of the US-led coalition using bombs, missiles and drones.

The Kurds in Syria have always wondered what is going to happen to them once the US no longer needs them as an essential ally against Isis. They are a community of some 2.2 million people who were marginalized and persecuted until the uprising against the Syrian regime in 2011. The Syrian army withdrew in 2012 from Kurdish territory and the Kurds established what they called Rojava, linking up Kurdish enclaves in a wedge of territory in north east Syria south of the Turkish border. In 2014, the Kurds were attacked by Isis who almost captured the Kurdish city of Kobani, but were defeated after massive intervention by the US air force. The Pentagon had long been looking in vain for an ally on the ground in Syria and in the YPG it found one: the US-Kurdish alliance has been highly successful, but could now be a victim of its own success.

The Kurds are today operating in Sunni Arab areas that they cannot hope to retain permanently. They have pushed some SDF units further south downriver on the Euphrates into Deir Ezzor province where they risk colliding with the Syrian army coming from the west. Isis has retreated to this area which produces half of Syria's oil production.

Raqqa is about to fall – and once more, its imminent collapse has been brought about by Isis fighters who chose not to fight to the death. The Syrian Democratic Forces (SDF) – which is mostly Kurdish, is definitely not democratic and would have no force without US airpower – believe that they might hold the entire city within 24 hours and would thus erase the Isis 'capital' in Syria.

But the reports of more than at least 275 Isis fighters who are said to be Syrian and who have apparently been freed will greatly concern the Syrian government and army. Will they be allowed to wander into the Syrian Desert and stage attacks on the Syrian army? Or go to join their comrades in Deir Ezzor, the government-held city which has still not been taken in its entirety by Syrian troops?

This is the second time in a week that Isis have surrendered en masse – the Kurdish-led 'SDF' says that only foreign fighters remain in Raqqa – and the assumption must be that ISIS is either content to give up the battle and fight again another day, or simply to find their way home and give up the struggle. The latter may be the more likely. But the Syrian government army is also only a few miles from Raqqa and has its own liaison office with the Kurds of the 'SDF' – and with the Russian air force – in a small location close to the Euphrates river. They will want to know details of this large-scale surrender – or large-scale freeing of prisoners which seems to be what is happening.

Isis is facing total defeat - but has been beaten and come back before

The fighters are thought to have been taken initially to Hawi al-Hawa prison outside Raqqa where they are being interrogated – hopefully more humanely than were Isis prisoners captured by Shia Iraqi militias in Mosul. Raqqa's short truce also provided the moment for hundreds of civilians to flee the city, including the wives and children of fighters. So it seems that all the visions of heroic death and paradise conjured up by Isis leaders – many of whom are themselves dead – no longer appear to be worthy of their fighters.

The mere fact that they will talk to their opponents is an extraordinary step, although there is a third example of such a surrender: when the Syrians and Hezbollah fighters on Syria's border with Lebanon allowed Isis fighters and other Islamists to leave the hills above the Lebanese town of Ersal earlier this year. Isis is facing near total defeat in Iraq and Syria – but it has been beaten and come back before

Jihadis have been preparing bunkers with weapons caches in the desert, ready to wait out the storm.Isis has fought desperately and skilfully to hold the Syrian city of Raqqa, under siege by Kurdish-led forces for more than four months, but will soon lose it in the latest defeat for the Islamic fundamentalist movement. Little is left today of the Caliphate declared in 2014, which once ruled most of western Iraq and eastern Syria?

Isis battled far longer than anybody expected for Mosul and Raqqa, but had to fight on multiple fronts against its many enemies and, above all, against the immense firepower of the US, Russian and allied air forces as well as conventional artillery. It was only by pounding large parts of both cities into rubble that the Iraqi security forces and the Syrian Democratic Forces (SDF) have been able to prevail.

. Hard fought though the battles have been, there is no doubt who has won them and co
Hard fought though the battles have been, there is no doubt that has won them and come out on top. Significantly, Isis has not put up much of a fight for Tal Afar west of Mosul or Hawija to the south, which were long term Isis strongholds. Only in Deir ez-Zor province on the Euphrates downriver from Raqqa are there signs that Isis has combat units capable of launching

successful counter-attacks. One of these ejected Syrian government forces from Mayadin, a small city in eastern Syria in the last few days.. I

Fighting worst since battle for Aleppo

A key factor has been the intervention of regional and world powers, including Iran, Russia, Saudi Arabia and the United States. Their military, financial and political support for the government and opposition has contributed directly to the intensification and continuation of the fighting, and turned Syria into a proxy battleground.

External powers have also been accused of fostering sectarianism in what was a broadly secular state, pitching the country's Sunni majority against the president's Shia Alawite sect. Such divisions have encouraged both sides to commit atrocities that have not only caused loss of life but also torn apart communities, hardened positions and dimmed hopes for a political settlement.

Jihadist groups have also seized on the divisions, and their rise has added a further dimension to the war. Hayat Tahrir al-Sham, an alliance formed by what was once the al-Qaeda-affiliated al-Nusra Front, controls large parts of the north-western province of Idlib.

Meanwhile, so-called Islamic State (IS), which controls large swathes of northern and eastern Syria, is battling government forces, rebel brigades and Kurdish militias, as well as facing air strikes by Russia and a US-led multinational coalition. As many as 10 hospitals have reportedly been damaged during the last 10 days, cutting hundreds of thousands of people off from access to basic healthcare. The ICRC said the fighting around

the eastern city of Deir al-Zour - where Syrian pro-government forces, helped by the Russian military and Iranian-backed militias, and the US-backed Syrian Democratic Forces (SDF) alliance are battling the jihadist group Islamic State (IS) - is endangering water supplies there.

With swelling numbers of civilians fleeing military operations, humanitarian organisations were struggling to provide water, food and basic hygiene, it added.

The Syrian Observatory for Human Rights has said at least 3,000 people, including 955 civilians, were killed during September, making it the deadliest month of the conflict so far this year. More than 70% of the civilians were killed in air strikes, according to the UK-based monitoring group.

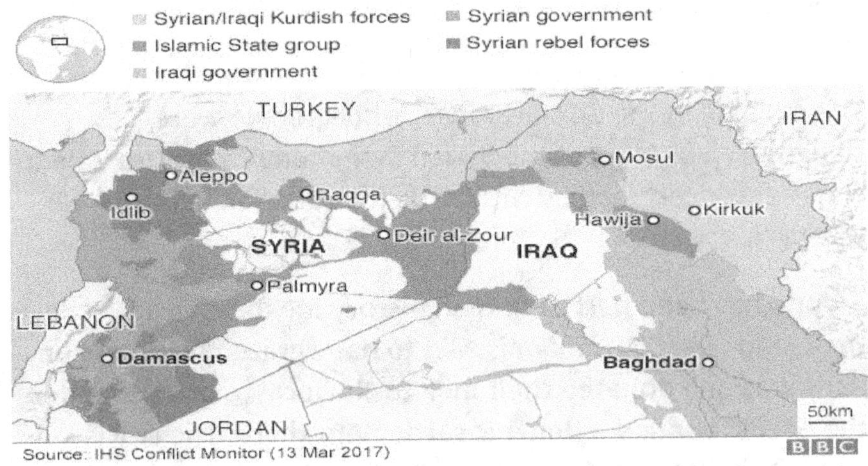

Aleppo: the guilt, the resentment, the indifference

The Battle for Aleppo, Syria's Stalingrad, Ends

Supporters of Syria's President Bashar al-Assad tour the streets in celebration of what they say is the Syrian army's victory against the rebels in Aleppo [Reuters]

It seems the only way to isolate yourself from the tragedies of Aleppo is to be in Damascus.

While most of my Syrian friends abroad are posting about Aleppo on social media, my friends in Damascus are talking about late night pizzas, posting photos of graduation ceremonies and of the wet grey asphalt after a short night rain, and celebrating autumn. Maybe the only way to shade your eyes from this calamity is to care about your own survival.

The evening of the 14 December, while people were slaughtered in Aleppo, the Syrian Symphony Orchestra held a classical concert lead by Missak Baghboudarian in Damascus Opera House.

Aleppo has been part of human history for some five thousand years. Abraham is said to have grazed his sheep on its slopes and donated their milk to the local poor. Alexander the Great founded a Hellenic settlement there. The city is cited in the Book of Samuel and Psalm 60, and for centuries its residents reflected the three great Abrahamic faiths. It was at one end of the ancient Silk Road, and a major metropolis in

the many empires that conquered and ruled the region. Its medieval Citadel, pivotal during the Crusades, is one of the world's oldest and largest castles. More recently, Shakespeare referred to Aleppo in both "Macbeth" and "Othello."

The Battle of Aleppo, which since 2012 has pitted the despotic government of President Bashar al-Assad against an array of disorganized opposition rebels, now appears to be over. A deal to allow the safe passage of the last opposition fighters, their families, and any civilians who want to leave—an end to the agony—was brokered Tuesday by Russia and Turkey. "All militants, together with members of their family and the injured, currently are going through agreed corridors in directions that they have chosen themselves voluntarily," Russian Ambassador Vitaly Churkin told the U.N. Security Council.

The United States was not party to the deal, a State Department official told me. "We would welcome a ceasefire," he said. "But we're not sure about Russian intentions. Historically, they don't always mean what they say."

Much of the famed city, the largest in Syria, has already been destroyed. The Old City has been gutted. The destruction has been compared to that at Stalingrad and in the Warsaw Ghetto. In a crescendo of cruel air strikes, which have escalated since the summer, eastern Aleppo fell this week to the government forces holding the city's western half.

The savagery had become primordial. On Monday, U.N. Secretary-General Ban Ki-moon expressed alarm over reports of dozens of summary executions by government forces, hundreds of "missing" men, and atrocities against women and children during the final military push. At a special session of the U.N. Security Council on the Aleppo crisis, on Tuesday, France's U.N. Ambassador, François Delattre, said, "The worst humanitarian tragedy of the twenty-first century is unfolding before our eyes." The International Red Cross warned of a "human catastrophe" as Aleppo plunged into chaos. "Every hour, butcheries are carried out," the Syrian Observatory for Human Rights reported. On Tuesday, it said that some six thousand boys and men had been detained after fleeing rebel-held areas.

The fall of Aleppo is the biggest victory for Assad in the grisly six-year war, which has killed more than four hundred thousand people and left more than half of Syria's population, originally twenty-two million, dependent on international aid for daily survival. The odds were always against the rebel groups, which were outnumbered and outgunned by a government with airpower—and Russian, Iranian, and Lebanese Shiite forces to back it up. In the final days in the east, they basically collapsed.

"They don't have much time. They either have to surrender or die," Syrian Lieutenant General Zaid al-Saleh told reporters on Monday, as he toured part of the recaptured city. Bedraggled civilians—long under siege and without hospitals, since the last one was bombed this fall—fled eastern Aleppo in droves.

The Assad dynasty's conquest of Aleppo is a boon to the Russians, who covet Syria as their prime Arab ally—and for its Mediterranean port. Moscow may be gaming the Presidential transition in the United States, U.S. officials told me. It is trying to insure that Assad regains control over as much Syrian territory as possible before President-elect Donald Trump is inaugurated—to present the survival of the regime as a fait accompli. Iran and its Hezbollah allies are winners, too, albeit at a cost.

The loss of Aleppo is, in turn, a huge setback for the West, Turkey, and the Gulf monarchies, which supported several rebel factions with arms, training, or funds. For two years, Secretary of State John Kerry has been trying to broker a political transition that would include both the government and the opposition. As that effort imploded, he repeatedly met with his Russian counterpart, Sergey Lavrov, right up until last week, in Hamburg—in an attempt to negotiate a ceasefire that would allow the rebels and civilians a peaceful exit to a place of their choice. In the end, Russia managed to make a deal that excluded the United States.

The deepening tension between Washington and Moscow over Aleppo was reflected in an exchange at the Security Council on Tuesday. U.S. Ambassador Samantha Power rebuked Assad, Russia, and Iran. "Your forces and proxies are carrying out these crimes," she said. "Your barrel bombs and mortars and air strikes have allowed the militia in Aleppo to encircle tens of thousands of civilians in your ever-tightening noose. It is your noose. Three member states of the U.N.

contributing to a noose around civilians. It should shame you. Instead, by all appearances, it is emboldening you. You are plotting your next assault. Are you truly incapable of shame? Is there literally nothing that can shame you? Is there no act of barbarism against civilians, no execution of a child that gets under your skin, that just creeps you out a little bit? Is there nothing you will not lie about or justify?"

Churkin, the Russian envoy, countered that it was "very strange" that Power issued a statement "as if she was Mother Teresa." He added, "Please remember what country you are representing. Please remember your country's track record, and then you can start opining from the position of any moral supremacy."

Assad's restored grip over Syria's commercial hub—its New York—does not end the war. Farfrom it. The Syrian conflict has been increasingly multilayered. A variety of rebel groups—some nationalist, some local, some non-ideological, and some Islamist, including the most potent Al Qaeda branch, Jabhat Fateh al-Sham—still hold Idlib Province, in the northwest. Assad and his foreign backers are likely to try to win it back next. It may prove harder than Aleppo. Assad's army surrounded Aleppo and cut off its roads to Turkey, which had allowed the rebels to resupply and rearm. It will be much more difficult to do that in Idlib, on the Turkish border. Turkey would have to reverse its longstanding opposition to Assad and turn its back on the rebels.

A separate war is playing out in the northeast, along the Iraq border, which has been occupied, since late 2013, by the Islamic State. Much of the fighting there pits isis against other Syrian rebels. isis has lost almost thirty per cent of its turf under pressure from the Syrian Democratic Forces, a Kurdish-heavy militia, backed by punishing U.S. airpower. isis fighters have fought Assad's army in fewer places, such as Palmyra, in the central Syrian desert, which isis captured in May, 2015. The Syrian Army won it back in March. This weekend, though, isis proved that it can still surprise. As Assad's army ground away at Aleppo, isis recaptured Palmyra. Damascus was stunned.

The conflict also shows no signs of ending, because it has sucked in other countries, causes, competing political visions, and sectarian tensions. The balance of power in the Middle East—notably between regional rivals Saudi Arabia and Iran, but dragging in others—is also at stake in Syria, a prime geo-strategic property. Riyadh has backed several Sunni rebels, while Tehran has supported the government, led by Alawites, a minority linked to Shiites. The tensions are not just over religious dogma; they are also about competing political visions and interests in the wider Middle East. Neither side is likely to give up, even when its allies are weakened.

During the Obama Administration, a parallel rivalry has played out between the United States and Russia over Syria. That may change under Trump, or he may try to change it. But the President-elect is likely to discover that, by dramatically shifting course and agreeing to terms that favor Russia and keep Assad in power, he risks angering allies or endangering long-standing partnerships—including with Turkey and the Gulf monarchies—with their own interests in Syria.

Each layer of the conflict ultimately goes back to the original flashpoint, in 2011, when a group of teen-agers wrote anti-government graffiti on public walls in Daraa, a remote town in southern Syria, reflecting the spirit of the inspiring, if short-lived, Arab Spring. Their arrests sparked public protests that swept across the country. The regime's repressive response has since spawned a full spectrum of opposition not easily contained or pacified, even with massive firepower. Not one of the many Syrian wars can be solved without a political compromise among one of the most ethnically and religiously diverse societies in the Middle East.

"Without a political transition within Syria, the fighting won't stop," a U.S. official told me late Monday. "And, without a political transition, there's no way we can finish off the Islamic State."

The U.N. High Commissioner of Human Rights, Zeid Ra'ad al-Hussein, on Tuesday warned that the government's "crushing" of Aleppo may only encourage the regime to repeat the same strategy—including "the wanton slaughter of men, women and children"—elsewhere in Syria, notably in Idlib Province; Douma, near Damascus; and Raqqa, the pseudo-capital of ISIS. Even if there is eventually some kind of peace, it would be fragile, given the political animosities and human desperation produced by this conflict. Meanwhile, lands with Biblical history have been devastated. There will be little of Syria left, physically, for its people to return to not an environment offering much hope for real reconciliation.

Why are so many outside powers involved?

Russia, for whom President Assad's survival is critical to maintaining its interests in Syria, launched an air campaign in September 2015 with the aim of "stabilising" the government after a series of defeats. Moscow stressed that it would target only "terrorists", but activists said its strikes mainly hit Western-backed rebel groups.

Six months later, having turned the tide of the war in his ally's favour, President Vladimir Putin ordered the "main part" of Russia's forces to withdraw, saying their mission had "on the whole" been accomplished. However, intense Russian air and missile strikes went on to play a major role in the government's siege of rebel-held eastern Aleppo, which fell in December 2016.

Shia power Iran is believed to be spending billions of dollars a year to bolster the Alawite-dominated government, providing military advisers and subsidised weapons, as well as lines of credit and oil transfers. It is also widely reported to have deployed hundreds of combat troops in Syria.

Mr Assad is Iran's closest Arab ally and Syria is the main transit point for Iranian weapons shipments to the Lebanese Shia Islamist movement Hezbollah, which has sent thousands of fighters to support government forces.

The US, which says President Assad is responsible for widespread atrocities, has provided only limited military assistance to "moderate" rebel groups, fearful that advanced weapons might end up in the hands of jihadists. The US has conducted air strikes on IS in Syria since September 2014, and, in the first intentional attack on Syria itself, hit an air base which it said was behind a deadly chemical attack, in April 2017.

Sunni-ruled Saudi Arabia, which is seeking to counter the influence of its rival Iran, has been a major provider of military and financial assistance to the rebels, including those with Islamist ideologies.

Turkey is another staunch supporter of the rebels. However, it has sought to contain the Kurdish Popular Protection Units (YPG) militia whose fighters are battling IS as part of the US-backed Syrian Democratic Forces (SDF) alliance. Ankara accuses the YPG of being an extension of the banned Turkish Kurdistan Workers' Party (PKK).

In August 2016, Turkish troops backed a rebel offensive to drive IS militants out of one of the last remaining stretches of the Syrian side of the border not controlled by the Kurds. Since then, they have taken control of some 2,000 sq km (772 sq miles) of territory, according to the Turkish military, and forced the US to deploy troops to the SDF-controlled town of Manbij to prevent clashes.

Why is Russia engaged in Aleppo?

Russia has launched a major new assault on what it calls "terrorist targets" in Syria as a brief calm around Aleppo is shattered by devastating air strikes.

Moscow says its first warplanes to take off from its aircraft carrier now stationed off the Syrian coast did not target Aleppo itself.

But Russia's intensifying intervention could be a game changer in the protracted battle to control this strategic city and the momentum in this brutal war. The timing was expected: in a few months time a new President, with a new Syria policy, takes over in Washington.

It was Russia's sudden decision in September 2015 to intervene militarily in Syria which marked the start of a decisive shift in the course of a brutal war which has come to define Syria.

Moscow has long-standing links to Syria, with many Syrian military officers trained and equipped by their Russian friends.

But its decision to significantly boost its military, political, and moral support to Damascus did nothing less than rescue depleted Syrian forces from collapse on significant front lines under grinding pressure from an array of opposition forces.

On a visit to Damascus shortly after Russia entered the fray, Syrian soldiers and officials hailed their strong cultural affinity with the Russians, as well as their gratitude in their hour of need.

Russian officials often say their intervention "stopped the black flags" of so-called Islamic State (IS) from being raised in the Syrian capital. The threat posed by Islamic extremists is very real. But strengthening President Assad was a winning move for Moscow on many fronts.

It transformed Russia from a minor actor on the Syrian stage to the lead player which continues to resonate across the region.

American officials warned a year ago that Russia's gambit would suck it into another Afghanistan quagmire which ended in humiliating and costly defeat during the Cold War.

But even Arab allies of the Syrian opposition have at times privately expressed admiration for President Vladimir Putin's muscular backing for an ally, at so far limited cost.

Russia's assets in Syria centre on its port at Tartus, its only seaport along the Mediterranean, as well as its newly established Khmeimim air base in the north-west, its only airfield in the Middle East.

Russia's parliament ratified an open-ended agreement to **approve the base which revealed what had been a secret pact** a year earlier to give Russia carte blanche to move personnel and cargo in and out of Syria, without inspection or interruption by Syrian authorities.

Over the past year more troops and considerable firepower, including advanced missile systems, have been moved onto the battlefield. Russian media have also reported the presence of Russian Special Forces as well as thousands of Russians working for military companies.

Russia and its Syrian ally cast their alliance as the winning team in the fight against IS. The capture of the ancient city of Palmyra last March - where Russia has now established a military post - is proof of that. But Western militaries and diplomats repeatedly accuse Moscow of targeting opposition groups backed by the West, as well as attacking schools and hospitals which put civilians in harm's way.

Accusations of possible war crimes are now a constant refrain.

The Syrian leader has long been a shrewd operator when it comes to playing his foreign friends off each other.

For Russia, this new projection of military power is about more than just Syria. It's one axis in a broader geopolitical battle to take what it sees as its rightful place at the world's top tables, on equal par with the power and prestige of the United States.

Endless talks with US Secretary of State John Kerry about finding a negotiated way out in Syria masked the quest for another prize - military to military co-operation, including intelligence sharing, which the Pentagon balks at.

For Russia, the redrawing of the map stretches to Ukraine and beyond in Moscow's new Cold War tensions with Nato nations.

Russia and Iran are on the same side in this war, along with Lebanese Hezbollah forces, and a dizzying array of fighters from far and wide including Iraqis and Afghans.

Iran's interests are different but no less essential: preserving its land corridor and access to Hezbollah in neighbouring Lebanon, protecting Shia shrines, and consolidating its growing geopolitical sway across the region at the expense of powerful Sunni rivals such as Saudi Arabia.

Both Iran and Russia have the back as well as the ear of President Assad, but not his complete acquiescence.

The Syrian leader has long been a shrewd operator when it comes to playing his foreign friends off each other.

When President Putin suddenly announced last March that he was pulling out "the main part" of Russian forces in Syria, talk in Damascus immediately turned to how Iran would fill any vacuum.

There has long been intense speculation over whether President Assad's most crucial allies would eventually try to nudge him aside for another less controversial strong man.

But they continue to insist the Syrian leader still commands popular support. For now, it suits them to keep him in charge.

And now US President-elect Donald Trump looks set to join this axis, at least in the fight against IS and the group once

known as the Nusra Front which has been linked to al-Qaeda.
President Assad has already called Mr Trump a "natural ally".

President Putin gambled last year when he entered Syria's
great game. Western leaders often say he played a weak
hand, and admit he's played it well - at least where it matters
to him, and his allies.

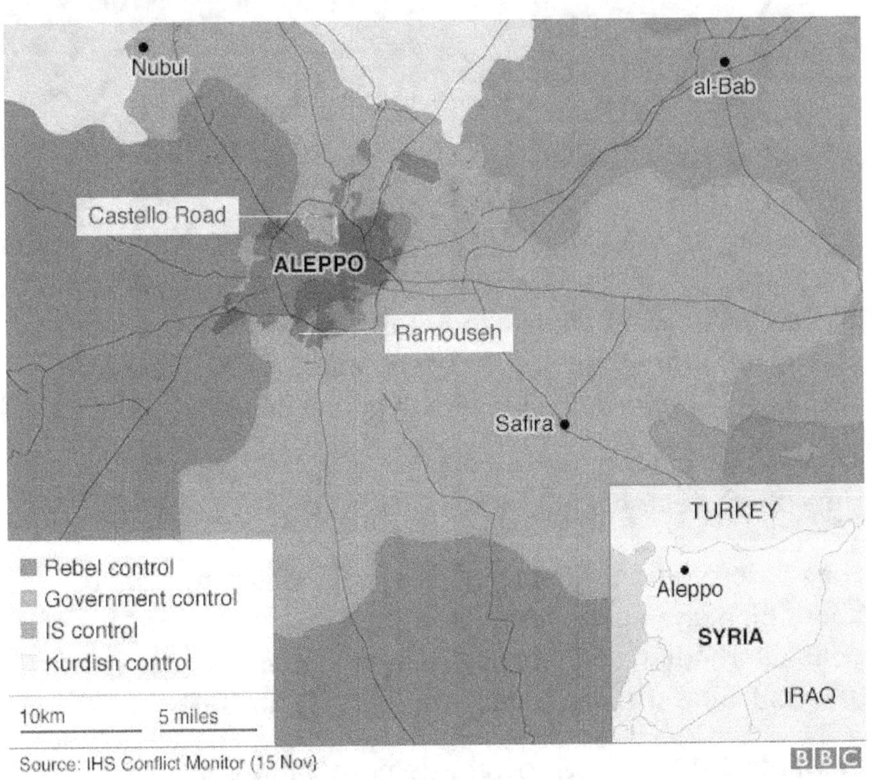

Why is there a war in Syria?

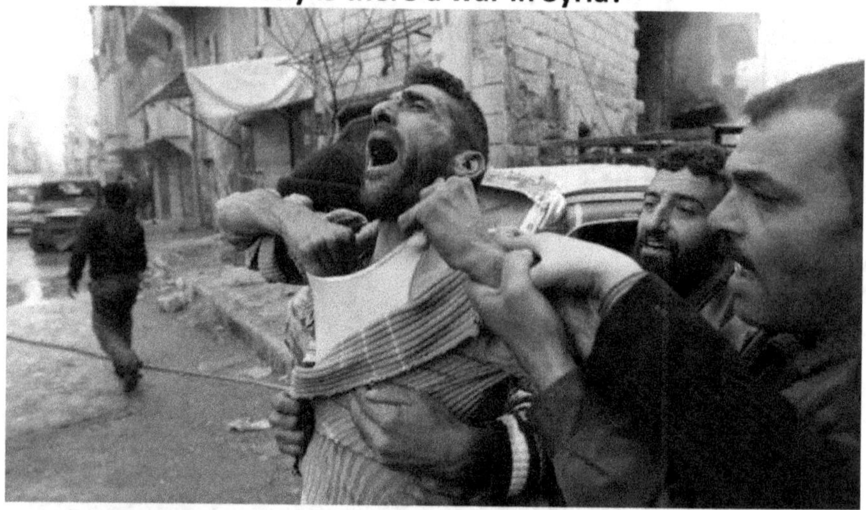

s What began as a peaceful uprising against Syria's President Bashar al-Assad six years ago became a full-scale civil war that has left more than 300,000 people dead, devastated the country and drawn in global powers.

How did the war begin?

Long before the conflict began, many Syrians complained about high unemployment, widespread corruption, a lack of political freedom and state repression under President Bashar al-Assad, who succeeded his father, Hafez, in 2000.

In March 2011, pro-democracy demonstrations inspired by the Arab Spring erupted in the southern city of Deraa. The government's use of deadly force to crush the dissent soon

triggered nationwide protests demanding the president's resignation.

2011 were suppressed by security forces

As the unrest spread, the crackdown intensified. Opposition supporters began to take up arms, first to defend themselves and later to expel security forces from their local areas. Mr Assad vowed to crush "foreign-backed terrorism" and restore state control.

The violence rapidly escalated and the country descended into civil war as hundreds of rebel brigades were formed to battle government forces for control of the country.

What impact what impact has the war had?
The UN says at least 250,000 people have been killed in the past five years. However, the organisation stopped updating its figures in August 2015. The Syrian Observatory for Human Rights, a UK-based monitoring group, puts the death toll at more than 321,000, while a think-tank estimated in February 2016 that the conflict had caused 470,000 deaths, either directly or indirectly.

Five million people - most of them women and children - have fled Syria, according to the UN. Neighboring Lebanon, Jordan and Turkey have struggled to cope with one of the largest refugee exoduses in recent history.

About 10% of Syrian refugees have sought safety in Europe, sowing political divisions as countries argue over sharing the burden. A further 6.3 million people are internally displaced inside Syria.

The UN estimates it will need $3.4bn (£2.7bn) to help the 13.5 million people who will require some form of humanitarian assistance inside Syria in 2017.

Almost 85% of Syrians live in poverty, with more than two-thirds of the population in either extreme or abject poverty. More than 12.8 million people in Syria require health assistance and more than seven million are food insecure amid rising prices and food shortages. Households spend up to a quarter of their income just on water. Some 1.75 million children are out of school.

The warring parties have compounded the problems by refusing humanitarian agencies access to many of those in need. Some 4.9 million people live in besieged or hard-to-reach areas.

Haran
Nineveh
ASSYRIA
SYRIA
Tigris River
Euphrates River
BABYLONIA
Babylon
CANAAN
Jerusalem

What's being done to end the conflict?

With neither side able to inflict a decisive defeat on the other, the international community long ago concluded that only a political solution could end the conflict. The UN Security Council has called for the implementation of the2012 Geneva Communique, which envisages a transitional governing body with full executive powers formed on the basis of mutual consent.

Peace talks in early 2014, known as Geneva II, broke down after only two rounds, with the UN blaming the Syrian government's refusal to discuss opposition demands.

A year later, the conflict with IS lent fresh impetus to the search for a political solution in Syria. The US and Russia persuaded representatives of the warring parties to attend "proximity talks" in Geneva in January 2016 to discuss a Security Council-endorsed road map for peace, including a ceasefire and a transitional period ending with elections.

The first round broke down while still in the "preparatory" phase, as government forces launched an offensive around Aleppo. The talks resumed in March 2016, after the US and Russia brokered a nationwide "cessation of hostilities" that excluded jihadist groups. But they collapsed the following month.

Turkey and Russia brokered another truce after the fall of Aleppo. In January 2017, they and Kazakhstan hosted the first face-to-face meeting between rebel fighters and government officials since the war began. That was followed by a fresh round of UN-mediated talks in Geneva, which UN envoy Staffan de Mistura said "achieved much more than many people had imagined we could have".

The fall of Aleppo means the government now controls Syria's four biggest cities. But large parts of the country are still held by other armed groups.

Rebel fighters and allied jihadists are estimated to control about 15% of Syrian territory, according to the Syrian Observatory for Human Rights.

US officials said in early December 2016 that there were 50,000 or more "moderate" rebels, concentrated in the north-western province of Idlib and the western Aleppo countryside.

Rebels also control smaller areas in the central province of Homs, the southern provinces of Deraa and Quneitra, and the eastern Ghouta agricultural belt outside Damascus.

Kurdish forces, who say they support neither the government nor the opposition, meanwhile control much of Syria's border with Turkey, as well as a large part of the country's north-east.

And although they have suffered extensive losses in the past two years, IS militants still hold large parts of central and northern Syria, including the city of Raqqa.

The armed opposition in Syria was under the direct command of foreign governments from the early years of the conflict

A television interview of a top Qatari official confessing the truth behind the origins of the war in Syria is going viral across Arabic social media during the same week a leaked top secret NSA document was published which confirms that the armed opposition in Syria was under the direct command of foreign governments from the early years of the conflict.

And according to a well-known Syria analyst and economic adviser with close contacts in the Syrian government, the explosive interview constitutes a high level "public admission to collusion and coordination between four countries to destabilize an independent state, [including] possible support for Nusra/al-Qaeda." Importantly, "this admission will help build case for what Damascus sees as an attack on its security & sovereignty. It will form basis for compensation claims."

In an interview with Qatari TV Wednesday, bin Jaber al-Thani revealed that his country, alongside Saudi Arabia, Turkey, and the United States, began shipping weapons to jihadists from the very moment events "first started" (in 2011).

Al-Thani even likened the covert operation to "hunting prey" - the prey being President Assad and his supporters - "prey" which he admits got away (as Assad is still in power; he used a Gulf Arabic dialect word, "al-sayda", which implies hunting animals or prey for sport). Though Thani denied credible allegations of support for ISIS, the former prime minister's words implied direct Gulf and US support for al-Qaeda in Syria (al-Nusra Front) from the earliest years of the war, and even said Qatar has "full documents" and records proving that the war was planned to effect regime change.

According to Zero Hedge's translation, al-Thani said while acknowledging Gulf nations were arming jihadists in Syria with the approval and support of US and Turkey: "I don't want to go into details but we have full documents about us taking charge [in Syria]." He claimed that both Saudi Arabia's King Abdullah (who reigned until his death in 2015) and the United States placed Qatar in a lead role concerning covert operations to execute the proxy war.

The former prime minister's comments, while very revealing, were intended as a defense and excuse of Qatar's support for terrorism, and as a critique of the US and Saudi Arabia for essentially leaving Qatar "holding the bag" in terms of the war against Assad. Al-Thani explained that Qatar continued its financing of armed insurgents in Syria while other countries eventually wound down large-scale support, which is why he lashed out at the US and the Saudis, who initially "were with us in the same trench."

In a previous US television interview which was vastly underreported, al-Thani told Charlie Rose when asked about allegations of Qatar's support for terrorism that, "in Syria, everybody did mistakes, including your country." And said that when the war began in Syria, "all of use worked through two operation rooms: one in Jordan and one in Turkey."

The newly released NSA document confirms that a 2013 insurgent attack with advanced surface-to-surface rockets upon civilian areas of Damascus, including Damascus International Airport, was directly supplied and commanded by Saudi Arabia with full prior awareness of US intelligence. As the former Qatari prime minister now also confirms, both the Saudis and US government staffed "operations rooms" overseeing such heinous attacks during the time period of the 2013 Damascus airport attack.

No doubt there remains a massive trove of damning documentary evidence which will continue to trickle out in the coming months and years. At the very least, the continuing Qatari-Saudi diplomatic war will bear more fruit as each side builds a case against the other with charges of supporting terrorism. And as we can see from this latest Qatari TV interview, the United States itself will not be spared in this new open season of airing dirty laundry as old allies turn on each other.

Iraq, Syria and America

A senior U.S. military commander said Tuesday that 4,000 American troops are on the ground in Syria, a figure far greater than the 503 personnel the Trump administration says are deployed there.

Army Maj. Gen. James B. Jarrard, who heads the U.S.-led Special Operations task force targeting the Islamic State in Syria and Iraq, offered the surprising figure while briefing Pentagon-based reporters via satellite from Baghdad.

When asked to confirm the 4,000 figure, Jarrard appeared to be caught off guard. He then apologized and said the number is about 500. Eric Pahon, a Pentagon spokesman facilitating the briefing, interjected moments later, insisting the number is just 503.

"The general misspoke," Pahon told The Washington Post after the briefing. "I don't know what 4,000 refers to. That's nowhere near an accurate number."

Yet it's long been an open secret that the Pentagon has far more personnel involved in operations against the Islamic State, also known as ISIS, than its publicly disclosed figures. Hundreds of additional American forces — including Special Operations troops, forward air controllers and artillery crews — moved into Syria to back up allied local forces as they prepared to assault Raqqa, which was the Islamic State's self-declared capital until its fall this month.

Earlier this year, teams of Army Rangers were rushed to Manbij for a mission the Pentagon called "reassurance and deterrence," which was intended to maintain peace between Syrian Kurdish forces who liberated the city and armed groups loyal to neighboring Turkey. U.S. commanders also routinely send attack helicopters into Syria and leave them there, sometimes for days at a time.

The Trump administration says there are 5,262 U.S. troops supporting war efforts in Iraq, though the number is believed to be much higher.

"It's widely acknowledged there are more than 503 in Syria and 5,200 in Iraq," Pahon told The Post. "These are our force management level numbers. They don't include temporary forces."

A U.S. Marine guides an M777A2 Howitzer to a firing position May 14 in Syria. (Sgt. Matthew Callahan/U.S. Marine Corps)

Jennifer Cafarella, a Syria expert at the Institute for the Study of War, said sensitivity over U.S. troop levels in Syria and Iraq dates to the Obama administration, which was determined to fight the Islamic State with a minimal American presence on the ground.

"President Obama," she said, "was forced to repeatedly scale up the U.S. role after it became clear that his initial strategy to partner with local forces could not generate the necessary outcomes without greater U.S. involvement. Whether or not Major General Jarrard's statement was accurate, the U.S was certainly drawn deeper into Iraq and Syria than it seems was originally planned. This troop creep reflects flaws in the design of U.S. strategy against ISIS that U.S. policymakers continue to fail to recognize."

These are not the only countries where the Pentagon appears to have manipulated deployment numbers. As the Wall Street Journal revealed in August, there are about 3,000 more troops on the ground in Afghanistan than the administration's official tally showed.

The Pentagon has faced growing pressure from Congress to be more transparent about the scope of its activities overseas, not only in the Middle East but also throughout Africa and pockets of Southeast Asia. Defense Secretary Jim Mattis has promised to comply, but Jarrard's statement Monday is likely to raise deeper suspicion among those who've renewed scrutiny of the military's sprawling counterterrorism operations since the deaths of four American soldiers Oct. 4 in Niger.

Some lawmakers were taken aback by the size and scope of U.S. combat forces deployed throughout Africa. About 800 Americans are based in Niger to run counterterrorism operations and to train and advise local troops, and hundreds more U.S. forces are in other African countries. Mattis was summoned to Capitol Hill along with Secretary of State Rex Tillerson on Monday for a hearing over whether to update the laws that provide authority to fight terrorist groups and detain militants on multiple continents. They presented a unified front, saying that is unnecessary. Both indicated the administration is concerned about new laws inhibiting the military's ability to target terrorists anywhere in the world.

It is rather the disintegration of the USSR that led to some former republics becoming nests of Islamist radicalism.

Syrian crisis: Impact on Iraq

The Syrian crisis, which began with anti-government protests before escalating into full-scale civil war, has had a huge impact on neighbouring Iraq. From its stronghold in the Syrian town of Raqqa, the 'Islamic State of Iraq and the Levant' (ISIL/Da'esh), which originated in Iraq, was able to over-run a third of Iraq's territory in 2014, sowing death and destruction in its path and leading to the internal displacement of over 3 million Iraqis today. It is estimated that as many as 11 million Iraqis – almost a third of the population – may need humanitarian assistance this year to deal with the effects of continuous conflict and economic stagnation. Moreover, a quarter of a million Syrians have sought refuge in Iraq from the war raging in their country. Most have settled in the Kurdistan Region of Iraq (KRI), increasing the population of this autonomous region by nearly 30 % over the past few years. The – mostly Kurdish – Syrian refugees were well received by the government of the Kurdish Region, which gave Syrians the right to work in the region and to enrol in public schools and universities. Nevertheless, the large influx of refugees has placed strains on the local economy and host communities, and on public services. Prices and unemployment have increased while wages have tumbled. Economic growth in the KRI has slowed, while the poverty rate has more than doubled. The international community has stepped in to assist Iraq in its fight against ISIL/Da'esh and to help the country deal with the humanitarian crisis caused by the unprecedented displacement of Iraqis, and Syrian refugees. As a result of concerted military efforts, ISIL/Da'esh now occupies less than 10 % of Iraqi territory. At the same time, funds and substantial amounts of humanitarian aid have been poured into the country, to support the displaced and facilitate their return to areas over which the Iraqi State has re-established control. The EU is a leading partner in the effort to mitigate the impact of the Syrian crisis on its Iraqi neighbors.

After Brexit, Chilcot. Britain, run by people who long presumed to teach the world the finer points of governance, is in danger of becoming a byword for broken politics and gratuitous self-harm. This inquiry into the UK's involvement in the Iraq war, chaired by Sir John Chilcot, a retired civil servant, has taken seven years and now its report finally appears, 13 years after the US-British invasion, in 12 volumes running to 2.6m words.

It is hard to imagine how much more damage can be done to the tarnished reputations of Tony Blair, former prime minister, and his lieutenants, or whether any inquiry can capture the toxic mix of naivety, vanity and obtuseness that impelled this misadventure when the UK decided to go to war alongside President George W Bush.

Yet whatever Chilcot establishes, there are at least three deeper truths about Iraq — the geopolitical fiasco as well as the destruction of a state and society already brought low by tyranny, wars and sanctions — aside from the fact that the US and the UK started this war of choice with no more forethought than the Brexiters have exhibited.

First, Iraq offered the world a pitiless spectacle of the limits to US power (Britain's role was, in that sense, a sideshow). Obviously, America possesses military might in unique abundance. What it lacks is the ability to shape the broader Middle East, from Iraq to Afghanistan, or Syria to Libya. Conversely, the US and its allies do seem to possess the ability to help incubate worldwide security menaces. One result of Iraq is Isis, an even more savage iteration of jihadism than its al-Qaeda precursor, as we keep seeing, not just in Raqqa or Mosul, but from Dhaka to Medina, or Istanbul to Brussels; there is also regular carnage in Baghdad that rarely makes headlines.

It is no defence to keep repeating, as Mr Blair does, that the world is a better place without Saddam Hussein. Scores of little Saddams have taken his place. The casual upending of a millennium-old balance of power between Sunni and Shia triggered a sectarian bloodbath across the region and beyond.

Second, Iraq led to Syria. Sure, the Syrian civil war was detonated by region-wide uprisings against Arab despots, most of them aided and abetted by the west, leaving dissidents little space except the mosque to regroup — a chemically pure formula for the manufacture of Islamists and jihadis. But the sectarian parameters of Syria were set by Iraq. And western policy of outsourcing support for Syrian rebels to Turkey and Saudi Arabia not only helped create the vacuum into which Isis stepped but has helped pulverise Syria and Iraq, creating a real risk of regional implosion.

The frequent comparison of Iraq to the Suez crisis of 1956, the last hurrah of French and British colonialism, falls short. While Americans and Europeans have no plan to put a brake on the proxy warfare between Sunni Saudi Arabia and Shia Iran that Iraq set in train, they have managed to make Vladimir Putin's Russia, a predatory if subprime superpower, look surprisingly good. Third, the recklessness of Iraq followed by the fecklessness of western policy towards Syria has led to other inescapable if unintended consequences not least for the UK and EU. It is obvious not only in retrospect that the surge of refugees out of Syria, and the deal struck with Turkey to control it that appeared to offer visa-free travel in Europe to millions of Muslim Turks, were going to pump up the Brexit vote. In

Washington, London and other western capitals, the refrain that intervention in Syria is "too complicated", especially in light of Iraq, has become a political jingle. It obscures the fact that the west has been intervening, just not successfully. And it becomes self-prophetically truer as the shape-changing contours of the war keep getting worse. If only Messrs Bush and Blair had thought Iraq was too complicated.

THE ROOTS OF REGIONAL DISORDER

The Middle East is disordered, more so than at any time since the 1950s, when the Suez War, revolutions in a host of states, and the Yemeni civil war shaped the Arab state system we knew before 2011. Today's disorder came about because of long-building trends, and long-brewing problems, that undermined the authoritarian bargain by which these states maintained support from and control over their societies, and that produced widespread discontent that burst into the open in late 2010.

This is not to say that the Arab Spring caused the turmoil and violence we are witnessing now. It is to say that today we are witnessing the outcome of a longstanding crisis in state-society relations in the Arab world, one that took several decades to germinate, one that governments failed to address. This long-brewing crisis generated revolutions, to which many governments responded poorly: in ways that exacerbated societal divisions, further weakened and in some cases collapsed state institutions, generated violence, enabled the growth of terrorist movements, and has morphed in at least three countries into outright civil war.

It's no accident that Syria and Libya are the most disordered and violent parts of the region today. These are the places where leaders, having failed to act in a manner that could have prevented mass popular uprisings, then sought to repress their people through the use of force. Instead of restoring order, these brutal, power-hungry and shortsighted men broke their crumbling states to bits and drove their societies to civil war.

As institutions of basic governance and community order failed, those with guns to impose their will gained power. As the state apparatus turned against its own citizens, those citizens turned elsewhere for protection — toward identity-based, sectarian militias and toward extremist groups, often with horrific agendas.

The terrible choices of these terrible leaders, more than anything else, created the openings Al Qaeda, ISIS, and sectarian killers across the region now exploit for their own purposes, including to threaten American interests. And those same terrible choices that created a demand for militias in Syria has had a similar effect in the Arab states that are still standing populations fearful of spreading violence are demanding that their governments provide order and security even at the cost of freedom, accountability, or basic rights.

The roots of the region's upending — in the fraying and broken social contract — remind us that ISIS is not just an accelerant of chaos but is also a symptom of an underlying disorder. It is not the cause and not the disease. Where leaders have the will and capacity to govern without violence, where citizens are active participants in public life, and where state institutions respond to citizens' needs and are accountable to the public, terrorism may be a fringe phenomenon but will not be a dire threat.

The broken state-society relationship must be addressed if the region is to return to some form of stability. This has important implications for U.S. policy now, as the coalition pushes back ISIS in Iraq, and a coalition of extremist rebels in Syria pushes back Bashar al-Assad's forces in Syria.

With the breakdown of states, we also witnessed the breakdown of the regional order that had been in place more or less since the end of World War II. I don't think it's appropriate to talk about the end of Sykes-Picot, because what we are dealing with is not really about borders – and changing borders is no magic bullet for resolving the existing inter-communal conflicts.

These cross-cutting conflicts draw the states of the region into shifting coalitions in different arenas.

The American public, President Obama last year reversed his effort to "rebalance" America's foreign policy focus away from the Middle East, and re-committed American blood and treasure to a fight against violent extremism in the heart of the Arab world. This reversal, not two years after the United States had withdrawn its last soldiers from Iraq, was driven by a recognition that the spillover from the Syrian civil war could no longer be contained, and by the horrific video-broadcast beheadings of two American civilians by the so-called Islamic State group. But Obama's new commitment to the Middle East is fraught with uncertainties that are already provoking anxiety, both in the United States and in the region itself.

The first uncertainty is whether the coalition military commitment is sufficient to achieve the goals President Obama laid out in September – to degrade, defeat, and ultimately destroy the movement dubbed the Islamic State of Iraq and Syria, or ISIS.

Already the United States has had to send more military advisers than initially planned to support a decimated and demoralized Iraqi army. Already, the Iraqi government has given non-state militias, some under Iranian influence, a large role in the fight in ways that have exacerbated Sunni anxieties, and undermined the ability to peel local support and acquiescence among Iraqi Sunnis away from ISIS. That said, the operation in Tikrit last month, in which Iranian-supported militias failed and the Iraqi government relied on American air support for victory, showed the limits of Iranian influence in the Iraqi fight against ISIS, and showed the wisdom of a U.S. strategy that allows the Iraqi government the space to own responsibility for its own choices in this battle for its territory and for the hearts and minds of its population. However, this strategy ultimately stands or falls on Iraqi Prime Minister Abadi's ability to move forward with the kind of political and security steps that will build the confidence of Iraq's Sunnis in the Iraqi state.

A regular stream of news reporting suggests that U.S. efforts to equip and train cooperative Syrian opposition forces is only slowly taking shape, and will take more than a year, perhaps two or more, to have any meaningful battlefield impact. Meanwhile, recent reports suggest that a coalition of more extreme Islamist groups, including Jabhat al-Nusra, is successfully routing Syrian military forces in Idlib province (whether they can hold this territory is another question).

If Assad rallies, this war of attrition between him and the Islamist opposition forces could drag on for a long time, with mounting human cost and mounting spillover to neighboring states like Lebanon and Jordan. If somehow Assad is defeated, or pushed back to a narrow area around Damascus and Latakia, then the extremist rebels will have won the day, and they are unlikely to cede political authority to more moderate forces who did not do the fighting, nor to exiles, nor to Syria's remaining beleaguered liberals.

A second uncertainty is whether, even should the military campaign succeed, the necessary politics and diplomacy will follow to restore stability to these two broken states. If Arabs and Kurds, with U.S. air support, successfully push back ISIS in Iraq, can Iraq's distrustful ethnic and sectarian groups work together well enough to hold the country together? Prime Minister al-Abadi has introduced a National Guard proposal to parliament, but it is stalled, holding up something that restive and suspicious Sunnis see as a prerequisite for them to remain part of a Shi'a-dominated Iraqi state. Likewise, even should a moderate, US-supported Syrian opposition successfully challenge both ISIS and Assad in the bloody Syrian civil war, there's still little reason to believe that Iran and Russia are prepared to end their support for Assad, that Assad would agree to join a peace process that promises to end his reign in Damascus, or that Syria's fractious opposition factions could negotiate as a unit to achieve that goal.

THE BROADER IMPLICATIONS OF ISIS

President Obama was persuaded that ISIS presented a sufficient threat to U.S. interests to justify a sustained military response, ISIS is only a symptom of the underlying breakdown in regional order. The upheaval in the Middle East has likewise generated newly assertive regional powers like Turkey, new opportunities for longstanding troublemakers like Iran and Hizballah, and sometimes bitter disputes amongst Arab states like Qatar and the United Arab Emirates.

And, of course, this disorder is itself the product of the long-building pressures that generated the Arab Spring – the rise of a massive, educated, but largely unemployed generation of youth whose expectations for themselves and their societies far exceeded the real opportunities they could obtain given the arbitrary, repressive, and kleptocratic leaderships that characterized the pre-revolutionary Libya, Tunisia, Egypt and Yemen. While Iraq and Syria may get all the newsprint, marginalizing extremist movements like ISIS and Al Qaeda demands attention to other weak and fragile states in the Middle East and North Africa.

What that means is that, even as the United States focuses on arenas of intense violence, like Syria and Libya, attention must be paid to those areas where governing institutions are still functioning, albeit challenged – and we need to focus on helping institutions to listen to, include and serve the marginalized majority of the region, its young people.

SECTARIANISM AND CONFLICT IN TODAY'S MIDDLE EAST

In responding to the Arab uprisings, many governments found a sectarian narrative useful in justifying their actions and in rallying their populations. Iran of course saw a golden opportunity in the GCC crackdown in Bahrain in March 2011, and the Bahraini and Saudi media likewise waged a vicious anti-Shia campaign to label those protesting as agents of the enemy rather than citizens with a legitimate grievance. This sectarian narrative fit well also with events in Iraq, where Maliki was escalating his purge of Sunni politicians and military officers, and in Syria, where Bashar Assad, with help from Iran, was brutally suppressing mainly Sunni protesters. The sectarian narrative has helped both sides of this regional power struggle mobilize support, and also helped Sunni countries with Shia minorities deter, isolate, and punish any domestic Shia dissent. And in the face of the violence of recent years, that narrative of sectarian conflict is a reality for too many in Iraq and Syria.

The problem with governments wielding that sectarian narrative is that it becomes a self-fulfilling prophecy, and it actually increases the incentive on both sides for a real power competition to be fought both directly and through proxies. And we see that playing out across the region now.

Whatever motivated the Saudi-led intervention into Yemen, one consequence of this action is the hardening and extension of this narrative of sectarian conflict, aligning Sunni governments in a coalition that has defined its enemy in sectarian terms. I think we need to be concerned with the ways this development might exacerbate sectarian violence across the region over the longer term.

THE IRANIAN THREAT AS A UNIFYING FACTOR

The military operation in Yemen, while launched precipitously, not especially clear-cut in its goals or hopeful in its outcomes, seems to have served our Arab partners by unifying them more solidly against Iran than they were against ISIS, helping them to overcome internal divisions that had been sapping their capacity for effective collective action. That has obvious implications for the fight against ISIS in Iraq and Syria – especially given Saudi fears that the United States has ceded influence to Iran inside Iraq in order to fight ISIS. This presents a challenge for ongoing U.S. efforts to scale up its Arab partners' efforts against ISIS.

Some argue that this Arab assertiveness and fractiousness is a consequence of American disengagement – that if America had been more deeply invested in the region, especially militarily, our partners would line up and follow. There might have been a time, early in the Syrian conflict, when that was true. But today our regional partners are so caught up in what they view as existential struggles, that they are not necessarily interested in waiting for or following an American lead. In several instances over the last four years, the United States has voiced clear preferences and advanced clear efforts to resolve regional crises, and been rebuffed by regional governments – from Bahrain in 2011 to Egypt in 2013 to Libya in 2014. Regardless, today even a more engaged America that has reinserted itself into Iraq and is providing support to the campaign in Yemen cannot restore order without regional allies that share with Washington a clear view of the order they seek to impose, and that are prepared to set aside their differences so as to act together to impose it.

That's not what we have. In the contexts of the cross-cutting conflicts across the region, America's partners are so uncomfortable at the collapse of the region they knew, so fearful of the forces that collapse has unleashed, so mistrustful of one another's motives that collective action is very difficult to achieve or sustain. Even the much-touted Saudi-led coalition that intervened in Yemen was missing Oman, a major GCC member and neighbor of Yemen, and had several partners that were more symbolically than materially part of the fight.

Combining the shake-up in the regional balance of power, the sectarian dimension of regional politics, the anxieties of Sunni Arab governments, and the expansion of conflict in several regional arenas, we have the ingredients for proxy wars, miscalculations, and unintended or intended escalations of existing conflict. It is not an optimistic picture, and it does not bode well for the political compromises and wider reforms necessary to stabilize the region.

THE IMPACT OF A NUCLEAR DEAL

These escalatory dynamics within the region are likely to persist regardless to achieve an agreement that constrains Iran's nuclear program. In fact, whether there's a nuclear deal or not, I predict we will see a more aggressive approach by Iran in a host of arenas around the region, where the upheaval has given them greater opportunities than before.

If there is a nuclear deal, the hard-line elements within the Iranian regime, those most opposed to a deal, are also those with the greatest interest and investment in regional troublemaking. They are likely to use their ability to make noise regionally to try and compensate for the power disadvantages they see inherent in a deal – and they are likely to have a green light from the Supreme Leader to do so, because he will want to compensate them for their unhappiness with a deal.

If there's no deal on the nuclear issue, however, then the Iranian leadership will want to scale up its regional assertions of power for a different reason: in order to solidify or even strengthen its current regional power position in advance of whatever tougher American / Israeli / Sunni Arab efforts it anticipates to contain it.

Sunni allies are already upping their efforts in countering Iran regionally, as the Yemen operation and the renewed investment in the Syrian rebels demonstrates. Iran will have both the means and the incentive to respond in kind. This is a recipe for an escalator spiral, perhaps most particularly in Syria and Iraq.

What this means is that, no matter how much the US government asserts its primary regional interest in combating ISIS and Al Qaeda, our major regional partners will remain resolutely focused on the Iranian threat as their primary concern. And it means that, in reassuring and bolstering its partners as part of any Iranian nuclear deal, the United States cannot limit itself to the nuclear issue, or to traditional defense and deterrence.

No matter what equipment or systems the United States is willing to sell to its Arab partners, no matter what aid it is willing to provide, no matter what US assets the administration is prepared to base in the region – our partners are looking for a different kind of reassurance. They are looking to see the United States demonstrate its recognition of Iran's troublesome activities around the region, and demonstrate its readiness to push back against Iran's expansionism around the region. And the primary arena in which the Arab states wish to see that from the United States is in Syria.

Reportedly, recent gains by rebel forces against the Syrian military in Idlib province are the result of greater unity and strengthened capabilities due to more unified and concerted effort amongst the states of the Arab Gulf. If these forces continue to demonstrate success against Assad, they will be the most important players in shaping any post-Assad political order in what's left of Syria. We are still, tragically, a long way from negotiating a post-Assad political order – but to the extent that the United States does not have "skin in the game" on the ground in Syria, it will be difficult for Washington to exercise influence over either the Syrian rebels or their Gulf sponsors in shaping Syria's future. And the administration has resolutely resisted becoming more involved in shaping the trajectory of Syria's civil conflict, either directly or indirectly. This restraint is understandable, but if the current weakening of the Syrian military succeeds, or if the Iranian regime and Hizballah bolster Assad so that the conflict stalemates again at a higher level of violence, then the United States will be hard put to keep its focus in Syria on ISIS.

None of the foregoing is meant to suggest that a nuclear deal with Iran that meets the requirements laid out by the administration in light of the Lausanne framework is a bad idea. On balance, in this regional context, and even if a deal does not last as long as envisioned, it's a good idea to constrain Iran's nuclear activities to the extent possible and for as long as possible. The aspects of Iranian behavior that most trouble our allies will be there, and will likely escalate, irrespective of a nuclear agreement – and thus efforts to help expose and push back against those Iranian behaviors must be a key element of America's policy in the coming months.

In addition, the United States must attend now to the political components of its policy in Iraq and Syria. In Iraq that is primarily about how to help Iraqi Sunnis find their place within the Iraqi state, and how to help Prime Minister Abadi secure that space institutionally. Both Iran and the Sunni states have roles to play in stabilizing Iraq by ensuring that territory and people liberated from ISIS find a welcoming, responsive, and accountable government in Baghdad taking over.

On Syria, the United States must escalate its engagement with political forces that have been preparing plans for post-Assad Syria, and must also intensify its dialogue with its Sunni partners in the region to bridge gaps regarding priorities and strategy in Syria.

Finally, as discussed, the United States must keep firmly in mind that the underlying vulnerabilities that produced this upheaval and gave space for ISIS still exist across the region.

The United States must devote greater attention to supporting governments who are using political compromise instead of violence to resolve disputes, like Tunisia.

The United States should help local partners forge meaningful governance – not just a security presence – in ungoverned spaces like the Sinai.

The United States should help communities in the Middle East, through indigenous civil society, to build their own capacity for peaceful dialogue and conflict resolution.

Ultimately, building resilient societies and marginalizing ISIS, Al Qaeda, and their brethren across the region requires more effective, responsive institutions that can win citizens' trust and loyalty, and more fair and functional systems that can offer young people meaningful opportunities – not just jobs, but a chance to fulfill their long-denied dreams instead of placing their hopes in a world after this one.

To save Iraq, Washington must push for fair and credible power-sharing

US relations with its long-standing, historical ally the Kurdistan Regional Government (KRG) took a hit this month when Iraq's security forces and the Shiite militias of the Popular Mobilization Force (PMF) launched an offensive against the Peshmerga in the disputed territory of Kirkuk, with U.S. acquiescence. Washington's tacit support for the offensive stemmed from its policy of upending Iran-aligned factions in Iraq in the forthcoming parliamentary elections, namely by empowering Iraq's so-called moderate prime minister, Haidar al-Abadi. The idea, as it currently stands in Washington, is that the stronger Abadi looks to the electorate, the greater his chances of winning forthcoming elections.

But the elections are a long, volatile, and unpredictable six months away, and it may already be too late to sideline the Iran-aligned factions that dominate the PMF. Those groups are lionized by broad sections of the Shiite community, experiencing a meteoric rise following their role in the war on ISIS. Abadi, who came into office only three years ago without a popular and political base, cannot singlehandedly stop their ascendancy.

Enter the Kurds and Iraq's Arab Sunnis. Since 2003, no government has been formed without the Kurds, who have generally enjoyed the role of kingmaker as a consequence of the diffuse nature of power and politics in Baghdad and the confessional power-sharing arrangements. Ensuring the Kurds continue engaging with Baghdad and have a stake in the Iraqi state will be central to U.S. interests in Iraq: Absent Kurdish engagement to bolster al-Abadi's position, hardline Iran-aligned factions will almost certainly dominate the government and consolidate their hold on state institutions.

Ensuring the Kurds continue engaging with Baghdad and have a stake in the Iraqi state will be central to U.S. interests in Iraq.

Amid the tumult of the Kirkuk offensive and the frenzy around the Kurdish independence referendum last month, what has been remarkably absent from the discussion—and from U.S. engagements in Iraq—is Iraq's Arab Sunnis and their future. ISIS was born from the failures of governance and authority in the north. The marginalization of the Arab Sunni community, indiscriminate and disproportional anti-terror raids and arrests in Arab Sunni communities, and the lack of jobs and services provided an environment that was conducive to ISIS's emergence in 2014, alongside the sectarian rule of former-prime minister, Nouri al-Maliki.

Two competing orders that have shaped conflict and bloodshed in Iraq still remain very much in play: On the one hand, Iraq's Arab Shiite factions have instrumentalised the repressive rule of the Baath Party as a source of legitimacy, allowing them to position themselves as the liberators of the country and the guarantors of the post-2003 political order. Their identity and existence is based around narratives of victimhood and the notion of preventing a Baathist resurrection that would return the country to repressive rule. This narrative has provided Shiite Islamist parties and militias with the resources and capacity to mobilize cross-sections of the Shiite population.

Conversely, for Arab Sunni actors—ranging from political parties, to tribes, insurgent groups, and jihadis—the pre-2003 period is invoked to evoke memories of an era of Arab glory, free of militia rule, sectarian discord, and Safavid (Iranian) as well as Western imperialism. The latter narrative has enabled ISIS and its previous incarnations to swell their ranks and commit violent atrocities.

Kurdish statehood has been a long-standing, historical feature of Iraq's political history that does not necessarily determine the fate and legitimacy of the Iraqi state, even if it is disruptive and divisive. But failure to acquire the buy-in of Arab Sunnis will continue the two competing political orders that has resulted in hundreds of thousands of deaths, sectarian bloodshed and proxy warfare between competing regional powers.

Iraq does not necessarily have a sectarian problem but a governance problem; its ruling Shiite political class lacks vision and capacity to move the country forward. Baghdad's failures and the uncertainty of Iraq's future have even led Iraq's Arab Sunnis—once vehemently opposed to any weakening of the central government—to call for their own autonomous region akin to Kurdistan, one that allows them to manage their own security and resources within a federal Iraq.

The commentary on Kurdish independence has distorted the picture somewhat. The underlying problem that actually lies at the heart of the current conflict between the KRG and Baghdad— and between Baghdad's Shiite political class and the country's Arab Sunnis—is power-sharing. It is only through equitable, just, and sustained power-sharing arrangements firmly entrenched within Iraq's political system that conflict can be remedied and the Iraqi state can recover from its crisis of authority and legitimacy.

The United States can learn from past and recent mistakes: Fair and credible power sharing could have obviated the need for the independence referendum, but after events in Kirkuk, the United States now risks allowing Baghdad to exploit the momentum generated by the Kirkuk intervention and abuse America's willingness to give it the benefit of the doubt. Shiite militias and Iraqi security forces have moved against the Peshmerga to try and take control of Faysh-Khabur, strategically vital because oil from both Kurdistan and Baghdad-held parts of northern Iraq cross at a pipeline there into Turkey, the main route out of the area for international exports.

By controlling the border with Turkey, Baghdad could encircle Erbil and economically suffocate the KRG. However, the United States must prevent Baghdad from doing so to ensure that further advances do not result in implosion and a full-scale civil war that will almost certainly ensue if the Kurds believe their backs are to the wall.

Similarly, Washington failed to stand by the factions and fighters of the "Awakening Movement" project—a coalition of Sunni tribes and other actors that America backed between 2006 and 2008 to maintain security in local areas and combat al-Qaida in Iraq, in return for their integration into the state. Iraq's Arab Sunni-dominated heartlands in the north saw prolonged periods of stability, only for Iraq's Shiite political class to then renege on its terms and breed grievances that were then central to ISIS's emergence.

A decentralized Iraq that affords greater powers to communities and local actors could help enable the breathing room that allows the state and society to undergo a process of rehabilitation. The international community can adopt a dual-track policy aimed at strengthening local sub-state governance (through, for example, focusing on transitional justice and reconciliation, as well as by devolving reconstruction and development funds) but that also aims to strengthen institutions at the federal level.

The fragility of the Iraqi state and questions surrounding its legitimacy, along with sectarian conflict, will continue unless the United States asserts and re-calibrates its policies toward power-sharing arrangements. Those will constrain the space for violent and disorderly actors, including the Iran-aligned groups Washington seeks to sideline.

A blueprint for minimizing Iran's influence in the Middle East

Donald Trump would be making a serious mistake were he to withdraw from the Joint Comprehensive Plan of Action—the 2015 nuclear deal between various world powers and Iran—in coming months. This action, which Trump has threatened if Congress does not act soon to toughen our overall Iran policy, would be a much more serious blow to American interests and to U.S. global leadership than Trump's previous treaty-related decisions. Yes, he questioned alliances as a candidate, but he and his national-security team have recommitted to virtually all of them since January. Yes, he pulled out of the Trans-Pacific Partnership before the Senate could consider ratifying it, but Hillary Clinton had promised to do the same. Yes, he pulled the United States out of the Paris climate accord, another mistake. But that decision could be rescinded by a future American president, and the pact restored, with only limited harm done in the interim. By contrast, a unilateral abrogation of a painstakingly negotiated multilateral nuclear deal, blessed by U.N. Security Council resolution, would be a serious affront to international law, a sword in the side of the Nuclear Non-Proliferation Treaty, and a repudiation of the views of our core allies. Worse, it would probably be an irreversible decision, giving Iran carte blanche to resume many nuclear activities without constraint, and without any plausible way to restore the multilateral economic sanctions that had made Teheran cry uncle and negotiate the deal in the first place.

All that said, let's take up Trump at his word, and address his challenge. He is far from wrong to voice serious concerns about Iran's behavior throughout the broader Middle East. Many other Americans will reasonably wonder how we can reach an amicable agreement with Iran on nuclear matters while seemingly closing our eyes to Iran's lethal adventurism throughout the region. The latter Iranian behavior, which is ongoing and unrelenting since the JCPOA was signed in 2015, also makes the nuclear deal's "sunset provisions" even more troubling, since there is no sign that Iran is becoming less dangerous with time.

In fact, let's be even blunter and even starker: Over the last generation, no foreign government has more American blood on its hands than Iran's post–1979 revolutionary theocracy. It orchestrated the Marine barracks bombing in Lebanon in 1983 and the Khobar Towers bombing in Saudi Arabia in 1996. In Iraq since 2003, Iran's Quds Force has provided weaponry to both Sunni and Shiite insurgents who have killed hundreds of Americans. Tehran's ongoing efforts to foment trouble virtually wherever Shiites live in the Middle East—from Eastern Saudi Arabia to Iraq and Syria to Yemen and Bahrain and beyond—have worsened wars that have killed more than five hundred thousand and displaced more than 15 million since 2011. Its ongoing lethal support for Hamas and Hezbollah put Israel at constant peril.

So yes, we need a better strategy for containing and checking Iran, and it is needed now. If we are successful, Trump's mistaken threat may to blow up the JCPOA may be overtaken by events in what could become a win-win for the president as well as his critics.

However, the United States and allies struggle on other fronts. Both President Obama and President Trump have prioritized the fight against the Islamic State in Iraq and Syria over more comprehensive efforts to stabilize the two countries. Iran has profited from the security vacuum. The Yemeni civil war is yet another humanitarian catastrophe in the Middle East. The Saudi-led Arab coalition is stuck there in a quagmire. The longer that goes on the greater the human cost that provides ongoing opportunities for not just Iran but also al-Qaida and perhaps the Islamic State. The United States must begin to assert itself with the key actors to move the peace process forward. And Washington takes too minimalist of a role in helping strengthen key countries like Jordan and Egypt, which might be vulnerable to spillover effects from the region's wars that Iran helps stoke.

Pledge to maintain a U.S. military presence in Iraq for a longer period of time and extend the aid package for the country. Ideally, this commitment should have the support of the Gulf States and NATO allies. This type of commitment actually dovetails well with NATO's adaptive aspirations to help stabilize fragile states in the region. Iraq has suffered a generation of war and misrule, and years of low oil prices as well. Now, with Islamic State-held cities mostly liberated, the imperative of a successful rebuilding effort that engages all three major sectarian groups and prevents a return to civil war or the arrival of an Islamic State 2.0 is acute. A stronger, more stable Iraq will be much better positioned to resist domination by Iran. Given the stakes, and America's previous investment, aid levels comparable to those given Afghanistan or Egypt are in order. Engaging in this way can also enable the United States to help Baghdad keep an eye on the Iran-backed Shia militias as they are partially disbanded and partially worked into Iraqi Security Forces in coming months.

On Syria, an even tougher proposition, no single strategy is in order. Still, the United States and like-minded states—as well as global-aid agencies—need to help provide security and economic assistance to regions free of Assad's rule as well as the Islamic State. Some of these regions should be treated as temporary autonomous zones and help govern themselves as well. Additionally, more western and GCC military strength and support for moderate insurgents is needed in northwest parts of the country, such as in and around Idlib, where the Al Qaeda affiliate, formerly known as Jabhat al-Nusra, is still active. Otherwise, either the latter group or Assad's forces backed by Russia and Iran will be the likely victor.

Jordan, under severe threat with 1.4 million Syrian refugees enmeshed in its small population of 8 million, needs more help too. In addition to a better strategy to wind down the Syrian civil war, Jordan requires more financial support, especially for the kinds of economic development that will provide jobs to its young and reduce their receptivity to the kind of extremism that breeds terrorism, chaos and opportunities for Tehran.

To be sure, this is only a partial list. But Trump's unwise threats to the Iran nuclear deal can nonetheless help serve a broader purpose, or at least be prevented from creating another crisis, if we turn our minds in such directions.

The conflict in Syria and Iraq

Shawn Baldwin

The Syrian civil war began in March 2011 amidst the Arab Spring, when a wave of democratic protests spread throughout the Middle East. Protests began after the arrest, torture and killing of two teenage boys who had written anti-government graffiti.

Some governments in the Middle East responded to protests with compromise and democratic reforms. The Syrian government under Bashir Al-Assad responded by killing hundreds of protesters and jailing many more.

The war has now gone for over five years and become much more complex. Syria is now a place where rebel groups, terrorist organizations such as the so-called Islamic State, and international forces all struggle for power.

There are now 6.5 million people who have been forced to move within Syria. Over 270,000 people have been killed since July 2011, including 79,589 civilians. The situation has been made worse by environmental change, and conflict over food and water supplies.

Torture and chemical weapons have been used against people opposing the Assad regime and ethnic and religious minorities.

Kurdish people in northern Syria have experienced extreme hardship as an ethnic minority campaigning for independence from Iraq, Syria and Turkey. Kurdish civilians have faced persecution by the al-Nusra Front and ISIL as well as the Turkish government.

The international coalition led by the United States supports various rebel groups and conducts air strikes. The Russian government has remained loyal to its historical ally Syria and the government of Bashir al-Assad. The result is that war is prolonged by military aid from world superpowers while Syrians remain desperate for aid. According to the United Nations High Commissioner for Refugees (UNHCR), less than half of those internally displaced in Syria have gotten basic relief.

The Syrian civil war has created one of the world's greatest humanitarian crises. There is, unfortunately, no reason to believe that it will be resolved soon.

In Iraq, sectarian violence has continued since the removal of Saddam Hussein in 2003. This conflict has become worse since US forces left Iraq in December 2011, with the number of civilians dying continuing to rise. In 2014 there was a surge in radical Islamist movements such as ISIL which soon spread throughout Syria.

97% of the 250,500 Syrian refugees living in Iraq are based in Kurdistan, the northern Kurdish region of Iraq. There are currently 4.4 million people internally displaced in Iraq.

Recently the Iraqi government, with help from the US, successfully recaptured various major cities. ISIL have extended their area of control dangerously close to Iraq's three major oil refineries in Irbill, Baiji and Baghdad, and destroyed some of Iraq's most popular tourist attractions. This continues to have a devastating impact on the Iraqi economy, which is strained after more than a decade of conflict. The government remains in turmoil and the people of Iraq continue to struggle to live.

Cost of Iraq War

The Iraq War was a military conflict that lasted seven years (2003 - 2011) and cost $1.06 trillion. The Bush Administration launched it to eliminate the threat from Iraq's Sunni leader, Saddam Hussein. President Bush announced Hussein was developing weapons of mass destruction. The Iraq War was part of the War on Terror. That was the U.S. response to the 9/11 terrorist attacks by al-Qaida.

The War added more than $1 trillion to the U.S. debt.

That includes increases to the Department of Defense (DoD) and the Veterans Administration (VA) base budgets. The DoD base budget grew by $193 billion during the Iraq War. The VA budget expanded by $47.7 billion. Some of those increases are attributable to the War in Afghanistan.

It also includes the $819.7 billion in Overseas Contingency Operations (OCO) funds specifically dedicated to the Iraq War. That's more than the $738 billion in inflation-adjusted dollars spent on the Vietnam War. It's second only to the $4.1 trillion in inflation-adjusted dollars spent during World War II. For more on how to determine the actual cost of defense, see the U.S. Military Budget. The real cost of the Iraq War is more than the $1.06 trillion added to the debt. First, and most important, is the cost borne by the 4,488 U.S. troops who died, the 32,226 who suffered injuries, and their families.

More than 90 percent of soldiers wounded in Iraq survived thanks to improvements in battlefield medicine. That's up from the 86.5 percent injured who survived the Vietnam War. The higher survival rate also means many now must live with complex and grave damage. Twenty percent are being treated for Traumatic Brain Injury. Another 20 percent have either PTSD (Post Traumatic Stress Disorder) or depression. In addition, 796 suffered major limb amputation, while 235 died from self-inflicted wounds while serving in Iraq.

On average, 20 veterans commit suicide each day according to a 2016 VA study. The Iraq and Afghanistan Veterans of America (IAVA) found that 47 percent of its members knew of someone who had attempted suicide after returning from active duty. The group considers veteran suicide to be its number one issue.

Most American families did not feel the cost of the Iraq War at the time. First, there was no draft as there was in the Vietnam War or World War II. Second, there was no additional tax. As a result, those who served and their families bore the brunt. They will pay at least $300 billion over the next several decades to pay for their injured family members. That doesn't include lost income from jobs they quit to care for their relative. Companies, particularly small businesses, were disrupted by National Guard and Reserve call-ups.The economy has also been deprived of the productive contribution of the service members killed, wounded, or psychologically traumatized.

The Bush Administration wanted to eliminate the terrorist threat of Iraq's leader, Saddam Hussein. He was not affiliated with al-Qaida. But he was a Sunni Muslim who used violence to expand his power.

Saddam Hussein was Iraq's Sunni leader from 1979 until the U.S. invasion in 2003. The United States installed a leader from the Shiite majority. The Sunnis believe that Shiites (the majority in Iran) want to revive Persian rule over the Middle East. This Sunni-Shia split is the underlying driving force of tensions in the area. Sunni Saudi Arabia and Shiite Iran battle to control the Straits of Hormuz through which 20 percent of the world's oil passes.

The United States wanted to install a pro-U.S. government to stabilize the region. It thought that would defuse the unease between Iranian Shiites and Saudi Arabian Sunnis. It would also put pressure on Middle East kingdoms to allow more democracy. Then they would stop shielding al-Qaida and other anti-U.S. terrorist groups.

The Administration thought Hussein was a bigger threat than North Korea's dictator, Kim Jong-il. He could finance his terrorism with oil revenue. Troops never did find proof of chemical, nuclear, or biological weapons of mass destruction. But there was grave concern that Hussein was building that capacity. He had used chemical weapons on Kurds in Iraq.

Both parties in Congress, and 70 people of the American people, supported the war. Many thought we should have eliminated Hussein in the first Gulf War, after he invaded Kuwait. This concern escalated after 9/11. In addition, the War in Afghanistan overthrew the Taliban quickly. Supporters thought the Iraq War would be easily won. The Afghanistan War is a military conflict that began in 2001 and has cost $1.07 trillion. The Bush administration launched it in response to the 9/11 terrorist attacks by al-Qaida. The United States attacked the Taliban in Afghanistan for hiding al-Qaida's leader, Osama bin Laden. It was the kick-off to the War on Terror.

The war's $1.07 trillion cost has three main components. First is the $773 billion in Overseas Contingency Operations funds specifically dedicated to the Afghanistan War.

Second is the increase of $243 billion to the base budget of the Department of Defense. Third is the increase of $54.2 billion to the Veterans Administration budget.

Some of these costs are also attributable to the War in Iraq. But the true cost of the Afghanistan War should include the addition to these departments, even if some of the funds went toward both wars. For more on how to determine the actual cost of defense, see the U.S. Military Budget.

Iraq after the War

The Iraq war is not over even though U.S. troops are out. Fighting between the country's Shiite majority and Sunni minority continues. Sunnis are ostracized by the Shiite-led government. These frustrations drive the conflicts in Syria and Lebanon as well.

In fact, 2013 was the deadliest since 2008, the height of the war. The war had weakened al-Qaida in Iraq, Afghanistan, and Pakistan. But frustrations created a new terrorist threat. The Islamic State group promised a new homeland for Sunnis in the region. The cost to fight the Islamic State group in Iraq has spread to Syria, Jordan, and Lebanon. The Islamic State group took its war to Brussels, Paris, California, Berlin, and many other spots throughout the world.

The role of Russia in Syria

Moving towards the end of the war

Moscow in the Syrian war is acting like the maestro of an orchestra, aiming to control the pace of the battles and the distribution of power on the geopolitical map of the Levant.

Russia has decided that Syria has become a part of its political and military strategies, preventing the fall of a coherent governing system that protects the state and prevents the reproduction of the Libyan "failed state" scenario. To this end, and to maintain its influence in the Middle East through the Syrian window, Russia has worked on multiple fronts to ensure that it is not dragged into the Syrian quagmire, that the long war in Syria ends, and that the safety and long term security of its military bases on the borders of NATO Middle East – represented by Turkey – be confirmed.

Moscow showed its fangs to the Obama administration when they insisted on protecting al-Qaeda and other jihadists. The Russians used all kinds of modern weapons (appropriate to the Syrian war) to hit all of the United States allies and "protected" groups in Syria when these were working closely with al-Qaeda, and were benefitting from modern weapons, intelligence, finance and logistic supply from the countries of the region (Saudi Arabia, Qatar and Turkey). Moscow offered full air support to the Syrian army and its allies, and represented the spearhead of main attacks against the alliance of jihadists and the Syrian rebel groups. This led the forces of Damascus to a robust victory in the cities of Aleppo, Palmyra, rural Lattakia, and Damascus and other parts of Syria.

Russia has committed itself to strike any alliance of al-Qaeda and the armed opposition (even if these were not included in any peace talks) if these have the intention of violating the Astana-Kazakhstan ceasefire and preparing for a future offensive against the Syrian army. Moscow is asking Damascus and its allies to fight ISIS now rather than al-Qaeda, mainly established around Aleppo and in the northern city of Idlib, unless these insist on harassing the Syrian army positions.

The Kremlin rejected any Turkish proposition to advance into Kurdish territory because this is already liberated from ISIS. And it stopped Turkey dead at the city of al-Bab, preventing its forces from moving any further. Russia does not trust Turkey's intentions in Syria despite the recent visit of President Erdogan to Moscow (where warmth has returned to the relationship-for the sake of both countries' economies). President Putin was clear with Erdogan about his strategic alliance with Iran, despite his orchestrating terrorism whilst hoping to earn Trump's blessing.

Ankara may try to turn its attention towards Russia rather than the US in the forthcoming Astana 3 talks, hoping, probably in vain, to persuade Putin to choose to support Turkish forces against the Kurds in Syria. The military map has been already drawn, where Turkey has no place in the forthcoming war against ISIS- nor will she be allowed to venture into the area already liberated by the Kurds. Nevertheless, the Turkish influence is still needed against al-Qaeda due to the presence of several of its proxy groups in Idlib and around it, and due to the easy border crossings and benefits Turkey allows al-Qaeda to enjoy.

Moscow is expected to play an important role in the future of Syrian policy, imposing a political dialogue and negotiations between rebels and Damascus in Astana and Geneva. Russia is carefully avoiding the Afghanistan experience, unwilling to be drawn into a long war in Syria. This is one of the main reasons why Putin wants the end of the war as soon as possible. Already, the slogan of Assad should leave by military or political means is history: even the US is no longer asking for the departure of the Syrian President saying his fate will be decided "by the on-going political negotiations".

On the other hand, Russia has not interfered in the conflict between Israel and Iran (and its Lebanese Hezbollah ally). Israel was prevented from targeting any military force fighting alongside the Syrians, but, at the same time, Tel Aviv jets were given a free hand to bomb Iranian warehouses dedicated to Hezbollah in Lebanon or to the "Syrian resistance" in the Golan, a force which is preparing in the shadows for the post-Syrian war. Russia doesn't want to be part of this struggle and she has allowed both sides to sort out the rules of engagement on their own. Prime Minister Benyamin Netanyahu failed to convince President Putin and won't have a free hand to bomb Hezbollah and Iran in Syria as long as these are part of a coalition led by Russia to end ISIS and al-Qaeda in Syria. The war is not over yet and al-Qaeda has large forces in the north of Syria and others in the south. ISIS is still capable of causing damage, its fighters number several thousand in Syria and Iraq.

Saudi Arabia, Iran and Qatar role in Syria

The Middle Eastern countries understand today that Russia is planning to stay in Syria and will use all its powers to defend its interests. It is also clear that the US won't be able to alter Russia's decisive intention. Therefore all regional players are slowly pulling out, mainly following the recovery of the city of Aleppo by Damascus forces.

The UN envoy to Syria, Stafan De Mistura has clearly stated that the all parties should give up on the illusion of a possible military victory, engage in a global ceasefire, discuss the constitution (by the same Syrians), reconstruct the country and put an end to terrorism. There is to be no further talk about the fate of the Syrian President: a clear indication that the international community is prepared to give up on any group willing to continue fighting and that Syria is heading toward the end of the war.

This stand is sending a strong message to Saudi Arabia and Qatar that no more military supplies to rebels or jihadists will be tolerated, which means the end of the Middle Eastern countries' negative role. Saudi Arabia and Qatar never had a clear strategy in Syria except supplying weapons and finance for a regime change without necessarily planning for a new government or forwarding any kind of vision for the new ruler of Syria. A "failed state" was on the agenda of Saudi Arabia and Qatar even if that was leading to control by jihadists, al-Qaeda and ISIS, who would turn their guns, once they were strong enough, against these same Middle Eastern countries.

Speculation went viral in the media, claiming that Russia would ask Iran and Hezbollah to leave Syria as part of the peace process deal. This was wishful thinking since Moscow never raised the question with Iran and its allies. What makes this speculation unrealistic is the fact that only the Syrian government or President would ask his allies to leave the country. Moreover, al-Qaeda and ISIS still maintain tens of thousands of militants on the ground and the Syrian army alone, with the support of Russian Air Force, may not be able to cleanse the country of these. AQ and ISIS are equipped with a strong ideology, a driving force not present in the doctrine of the professional soldier: therefore, there is a need for similar ideologies so as to be able to fight back with the same determination.

Iran came to Syria in 1982 to respond to those who became known later as the Lebanese Hezbollah. Also, it is Assad who asked for the support of Hezbollah in 2013 when the situation became critical. Syria, Iran and Hezbollah form what is known as the "axis of resistance" where Syria fulfilled its deal by supplying advanced weapons to Hezbollah in 2006 (and continues to do so to this date) to face Israel. Therefore, Syria won't be in need of tens of thousands of allies once the war is over. The allies of Syria are expected to leave as fast as they landed in the country when Assad decides it shall be so, regardless of what Moscow or Washington wish.

Today, it is obvious that the Iranian strategy prevailed over that of Saudi Arabia and Qatar in Syria and managed to sustain a friendly government in Syria. Iran is also playing a positive role in the rapprochement between Baghdad and Damascus, resulting in military collaboration and the air bombing of ISIS targets by the Iraqi Air Force in Syria. Moreover, there is an on-going discussion between Damascus and Tehran for the construction of an Iranian naval base in the oil terminal port of Banias, 55 km from Latakia. If realised (it may take few years before it becomes operational) it will boost the crippled Syrian economy. Throughout the years of war, Iran has been supplying Syria with oil, mainly when the jihadists of ISIS and Al-Qaeda controlled the northern eastern oil fields. The so-called Islamic State in Iraq (ISI) is a deadly terrorist outfit that specializes in highly-lethal car bombings. ISI's traditional base are small Sunni towns in the Anbar province, but its unofficial capital is now Mosul, Iraq's third largest city.

Hezbollah

Hezbollah militants are present over the entire Syrian geography, supporting the Syrian army in its war against rebels and jihadists. Hezbollah believes Israel and the US, financed by Saudi Arabia, maybe preparing for another round of violence against the Lebanese group in Lebanon. Nevertheless, all facts indicate the opposite; if Trump is aiming for a spectacular victory, ISIS is much weaker than Hezbollah, easier to win over.

US prioritles in Syria are to degrade and contain ISIS and maybe al-Qaeda. To achieve this goal, Hezbollah forces are still needed. Moreover, the result of a war against Hezbollah, unlike ISIS, is not guaranteed. The tens of thousands of rockets and missiles held by Hezbollah can create real damage in Israel.

If Israel declares war against Hezbollah, Syria will take part as a direct player, dragging Russia with it. The destiny of the Syrian regime is linked to its victory in Syria. It won't hesitate to stand by those who fought with its army for years. Russia wouldn't want to see its plans in Syria collapsing when so close to achieving its goal.

The internal Israeli front is not ready to face a destructive war with Hezbollah, in control of between 150,000 to 200,000 rockets and missiles, according to Israeli officials.

The warfare experience gathered by Hezbollah in Syria made the group a challenging adversary when facing Israeli infantry. Hezbollah engaged in a different battle style against its fiercest enemies in Syria (ISIS and al-Qaeda) and showed itself to be fearless of death, unlike the Israeli army.

As long as the war in Syria was fuelled and active, Israel was feeling safe. Now that the beginning of the end is taking off, Israel is rightly worried. It took Hezbollah very few days to occupy the 600 sqkm city of al-Quseyr in 2013. How long it would it take to occupy the 2,380 sqkm of Galilee in a war situation? The war in Syria was highly beneficial to Hezbollah, despite the 1,600 men killed in the battlefield.

Syria looks both close to and far from the end of the war. There are still both military (against ISIS and al-Qaeda) and political battles (constitution, cease-fire, reconstruction) to be fought. Nevertheless, despite the US and Turkish occupation of Syrian territory which Damascus will have to face one day, there are clear signs that the war in Syria is on track towards its ending.

The US in Syria and the difficult choices

The United States has pushed hundreds of its Special Forces and elite troops into the north – east of Syria to maintain a military presence in the country and help the Syrian Kurds and Arab tribes fight ISIS[i]. The US forces are training, planning and supplying their proxies with weapons, offering air support and intelligence monitoring through SIGINTL (signal Intelligence) to observe and neutralise ISIS leaders and formulate attack plans for the city of Raqqa.

It is inevitable that there should be some redistribution of roles between the US and Russia over the attack to defeat ISIS in Raqqa. This is also manifested in the advance of the Syrian army towards ISIS-held territory[ii] in north-eastern Aleppo in order to stop the Turkish army and its allies from advancing beyond al-Bab city[iii] and to close the circle tighter around Raqqa by crossing the Euphrates River from the west bank. The Syrian army is aiming to liberate Deir Hafer and Maskana to complete its full control of northern-eastern rural Aleppo and cleanse it of any ISIS presence.Top military generals, Gen. Joseph F. Dunford Jr., the chairman of the Joint Chiefs of Staff, Gen. Valery V. Gerasimov, the chief of the Russian general staff; and their Turkish counterpart, Gen. Hulusi Akar met last week[iv] in Antalya and defined the limits the Turkish forces and their proxies can reach in Syria. It was clear that Ankara shall not be part of any attack against Raqqa and that its forces and proxies will stop at the limits defined by Al-Bab gates. Both the US and Russia want to avoid any Turkish-Kurdish clash in Syria, particularly as the danger from

Jihadists, ISIS and al-Qaida is far from being over, and that Kurdish forces still have a role to play in attacking ISIS around Raqqa.Aspects of President Trump's policy towards Syria are materialising, whilst there is a clear hesitation by the US administration regarding many other plans related to Bilad al-Sham during and after the war's end. Trump wants to avoid any military confrontation with Russia and acknowledge its presence and its role in Syria, useful also for combating terrorism. Moscow wants to end the war and look after its strategic interests by being present on the ground in the Middle East for many years to come, thanks to the Syrian window. It is also aiming to eliminate over 9,000 Russian nationals and various other nationalities fighting within the ranks of ISIS and al-Qaeda in Syria. It is in the interests of all the countries concerned to eliminate terrorists before they spread and leave Syria for other destinations and wage the jihad in some other place. This particular issue is driving the Russian-US coordination in countering terrorism, even if the US is still unclear about its own plans after the end of the war.

To-date, the intention of the US troops stationed in the north of Syria and its strategic objectives is still unclear. The presence of four US military bases and an airport under construction may be an indication that these forces are not willing to pull out any time soon. Leaving Syria won't be without a price and staying means the creation of a Kurdish Syrian enclave similar to Kurdistan in Iraq. This also means the Turkish forces will follow the US and keep over five thousand square kilometers annexed to Turkey.

It is also clear that though Trump is injecting more US troops on the ground, he is fighting, up to now, with Kurdish and Arab tribe's proxies. He may be aiming to register a "recognized victory" by defeating ISIS (the group is retreating on all fronts in Iraq and Syria, deprived of any support and with more limited finances) without diving into the Syrian quagmire. Such a victory may turn into failure if Trump decides to keep US troops there indefinitely once the Syrian war is over.

The question remains

Which forces will storm the city of Raqqa?

Twenty thousand Arab and Kurdish militants may be able to reach the gates of Raqqa and participate in surrounding it. The Arab tribes in the area will reject the control by Kurds of an Arab city. Moreover, there is no reason for the Kurds to risk their lives and lose hundreds or thousands of militants (hundreds of Kurds lost their lives to liberate Manbij city) to deliver the city of Raqqa back to the Arab tribes once it is liberated from ISIS.

Therefore, Trump will be facing a real dilemma, and will be forced to collaborate with Russia and its allies on this front against ISIS. Air strike coordination between Russia and the US is not excluded for the Kurds to reach one side of Raqqa and for the Syrian Army to storm the other side of the city, similar to the tactics used at Mosul (Iraqi Kurds were responsible for reaching the northern front of Mosul, contributing to surrounding ISIS). In this case, Trump won't be the only one to collect the victory, he will be forced to share it with Russia and work alongside the Syrian forces- unless of course he decides to put in his own US troops (several thousands) and accept the inevitable human losses! All difficult choices, but the collaboration of US, Russian and Syrian army forces in Syria is absolutely unavoidable.

Snow falls on Baghdad for first time in memory

January 11, 2008

A Hope of Peace

After weathering nearly five years of war, Baghdad residents thought they'd pretty much seen it all. But Friday morning, as muezzins were calling the faithful to prayer, the people here awoke to something certifiably new.

For the first time in memory, snow fell across Baghdad.

Although the white flakes quickly dissolved into gray puddles, they brought an emotion rarely expressed in this desert capital snarled by army checkpoints, divided by concrete walls and ravaged by sectarian killings — delight.

"It is the first time we've seen snow in Baghdad," said 60-year-old Hassan Zahar. "We've seen sleet before, but never snow. I looked at the faces of all the people, they were astonished," he said.

"A few minutes ago, I was covered with snowflakes. In my hair, on my shoulders. I invite all the people to enjoy peace, because the snow means peace," he said.

Traffic policeman Murtadha Fadhil, huddling under a balcony to keep dry, declared the snow "a new sign of the new Iraq."

"It's a sign of hope. We hope Iraqis will purify their hearts and politicians will work for the prosperity of all Iraqis."

The streets of the capital were largely empty as big, thick, wet flakes fell on Friday morning, a weekend day in Iraq. The temperature hovered around freezing and the snow mostly melted into grey puddles when it hit the ground.

But it was still lovely, said Mohanned Rahim, a baker: "This snow will bring pleasure to the people of Iraq. It's beautiful!"

Current Situation in Iraq

The US troops pulled out of Iraq in December 2011, marking the last stage of transferring full state sovereignty back into the hands of Iraqi authorities. The oil production is booming, and foreign companies are scrambling for lucrative contracts.

However, political divisions, in combination with a weak state and high unemployment, make Iraq one of the most unstable countries in the Middle East. The country remains deeply scarred by the brutal civil war (2006-08) that has poisoned relations between Iraq's religious communities for generations to come.

Democracy in Iraq bears the hallmarks of a political system born in foreign occupation and civil war. It is marked with deep divisions over the power of the executive, disputes between ethnic and religious groups, and between centralists and advocates of federalism. Yet for all its flaws, the democratic project in Iraq brought to an end more than four decades of dictatorship, and most Iraqis would probably prefer not to turn the clock back.

The effects of the Iraq War on the Middle East have been profound, but not quite in the way intended by the architects of the 2003 US-led invasion that toppled the regime of Saddam Hussein.

Top positions in Saddam Hussein's regime were occupied by Sunni Arabs, a minority in Iraq, but traditionally the dominant group going back to the Ottoman times. The US-led invasion enabled the Shiite Arab majority to claim the government, the first time in the modern Middle East that Shiites came to power in any Arab country. This historic event empowered Shiites across the region, in turn attracting suspicion and hostility of Sunni regimes.

Some Iraqi Sunnis launched an armed rebellion targeting the new Shiite-dominated government and foreign forces. The spiraling violence grew into a bloody and destructive civil war between Sunni and Shiite militias, which strained sectarian relations in Bahrain, Saudi Arabia and other Arab countries with a mixed Sunni-Shiite population.

Suppressed under Saddam's brutal police state, religious extremists of all colors began popping out in the chaotic years after the regime's fall. For Al-Qaeda, the arrival of a Shiite government and the presence of US troops created a dream environment. Posing as the protector of Sunnis, Al-Qaeda created alliances with both Islamist and secular Sunni insurgent groups and began seizing territory in the Sunni tribal heartland of north-western Iraq.

Al-Qaeda's brutal tactics and extremist religious agenda soon alienated many Sunnis who turned against the group, but a distinct Iraqi branch of Al-Qaeda, known as the "Islamic State in Iraq," has survived. Specializing in car bombing attacks, the group continues to target government forces and Shiites, while expanding its operations into neighboring Syria.

The fall of the Iraqi regime marked a critical point in Iran's ascendancy to a regional superpower. Saddam Hussein was Iran's greatest regional enemy and the two sides fought a bitter 8-year war in the 1980s. But Saddam's Sunni-dominated regime was now replaced with Shiite Islamists who enjoyed close links with the regime in the Shiite Iran.

Iran is today the most powerful foreign actor in Iraq, with an extensive trade and intelligence network in the country (though strongly opposed by the Sunni minority).

The fall of Iraq to Iran was a geopolitical disaster for the US-backed Sunni monarchies in the Persian Gulf. A new cold war between Saudi Arabia and Iran came to life, as the two powers began to vie for power and influence in the region, in process exacerbating further the Sunni-Shiite tension.

Iraqi Kurds were one of the principal winners of the war in Iraq. The de-facto autonomous status of the Kurdish entity in the north – protected by a UN-mandated no-fly zone since the 1991 Gulf War – was now officially recognized by Iraq's new constitution as the Kurdish Regional Government (KRG). Rich in oil resources and policed by its own security forces, the Iraqi Kurdistan became the most prosperous and stable region in the country.

The KRG is the closest any of the Kurdish people – split mainly between Iraq, Syria, Iran and Turkey – came to real statehood, emboldening Kurdish independence dreams elsewhere in the region. The civil war in Syria has provided Syria's Kurdish minority with an opportunity to renegotiate its status while forcing Turkey to consider dialogue with its own Kurdish separatists. The oil-rich Iraqi Kurds will no doubt play an important role in these developments.

Many advocates of Iraq war saw the toppling of Saddam Hussein as only the first step in the process of building a new regional order that would replace Arab dictatorship with US-friendly democratic governments. However, to most observers, the unintended boost to Iran and Al-Qaeda clearly showed the limits of US ability to reshape the Middle Eastern political map through military intervention.

When the push for democratization came in the shape of the Arab Spring in 2011, it happened on the back of homegrown, popular uprisings. Washington could do little to protect its allies in Egypt and Tunisia, and the outcome of this process on US regional influence remains wildly uncertain.

The US will remain the most powerful foreign player in the Middle East for some time to come, despite its diminishing need for the region's oil. But the fiasco of the state-building effort in Iraq gave way to a more cautious, "realist" foreign policy, manifested in the US reluctance to intervene in the civil war in Syria.

Sectarian Tension, Fear of Spillover from Syrian Civil War

The violence is spiking again. April 2013 was the deadliest month since 2008, marked with clashes between Sunni anti-government protesters and security forces, and bomb attacks against Shiites and government targets carried out by the Iraqi branch of Al Qaeda organization. Protesters in Sunni areas of north-western Iraq have been holding daily rallies since late 2012, accusing the Shiite-led central government of discrimination.

The situation is aggravated by the civil war in neighboring Syria. Iraqi Sunnis are sympathetic to the (largely Sunni) Syrian rebels, while the government backs Syrian President Bashar al-Assad who is also allied to Iran. The government fears that Syrian rebels could link with Sunni militants in Iraq, dragging the country back into civil conflict and possible partition along religious/ethnic lines.

Syrian conflict has now lasted longer than World War II

A horrifying fact regarding Syria that they have been through a seven-year war, longer the second World War. There had been a time of de-escalation in areas of the war-ridden nation; however, United Nations officials in a press release on the 9th of November now warn that the fighting is unfortunately returning to some of its bleakest days. The human suffering that was reduced to some extent during the time of de-escalation is once again particularly concerning due to the situation in Eastern Ghouta where conditions have worsened.

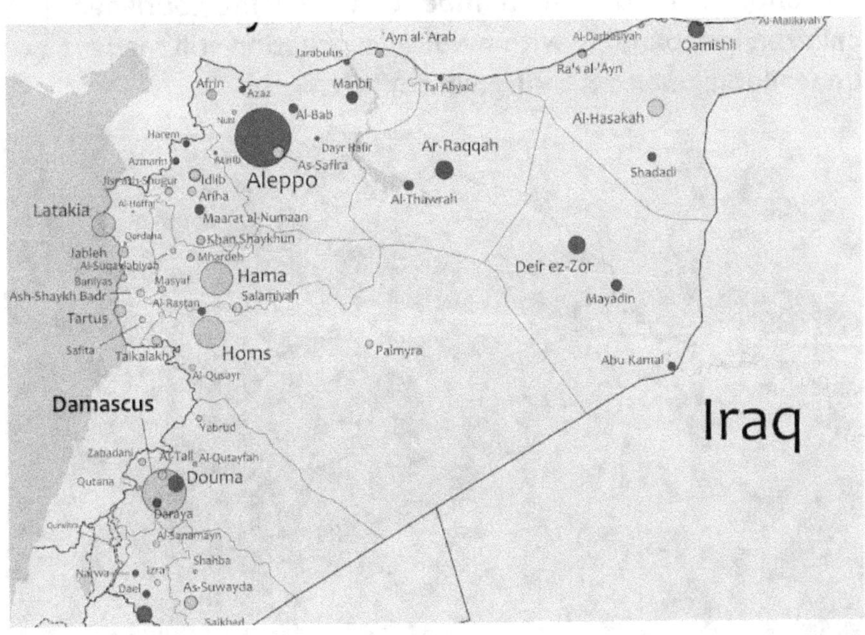

The situation in Eastern Ghouta concerns the fact that close to 400,000 people are living in besieged areas where food and basic health supplies are beyond reach due to the rising high prices of these fundamental objects. As a matter of fact, the UN believes the conditions in the area will become worse and difficult for people in the Eastern Ghouta area due to the oncoming freezing winter weather.

With little, if any, reserves, no heat in their houses and living amid ruin, it will be a horrific winter at the war threshold; the horrendous fact that the number of acutely malnourished children is expanding with medical evacuation still made unavailable due to the surge in conflict.

It is fraying as fighting spills across borders and international institutions built, at least in theory, to act as brakes on wanton slaughter fail to provide solutions. Populist movements on both sides of the Atlantic are not just riding anti-establishment anger, but stoking fears of a religious "other," this time Muslims.

These challenges have been crystallized, propelled and intensified by a conflagration once dismissed in the West as peripheral, to be filed, perhaps, under "Muslims killing Muslims": the war in Syria.

Syria overtook Iraq as the biggest and bloodiest mess in the Middle East a few years back. But while the spotlight has shifted to its neighbor, Iraq is still beset by ISIS and political infighting.

Tell Me How This Will End, War

In February 2009, less than two months after he took office,

In February 2009, President Obama flew to Camp Lejeune, N.C., and laid out his plan for ending the war in Iraq. He stood surrounded by camouflage-clad Marines, many of whom were just days away from being shipped off to Iraq or Afghanistan. He rose to national prominence in 2002 on the eve of the Iraq invasion by calling it a "dumb war; a rash war; a war based not on reason, but on passion; not on principle, but on politics." His candidacy hinged on his promise to end it as quickly as possible.

He was far from the first person to wrestle with the question of how to bring the messy, grinding fight to a close. In March 2003, with American troops bogged down by guerilla attacks on the way to Baghdad.

President Bush thought he had his answer the "Mission Accomplished" moment on the aircraft carrier USS Abraham Lincoln two months later, shortly after the fall of Saddam Hussein. "Because of you, our nation is more secure," he told the sailors on the Lincoln. But the war consumed Bush for the remainder of his presidency. Obama followed Bush into the White House determined not to let his presidency be defined by war especially not the one in Iraq, which had already cost more than 4,000 American lives and tens of thousands of Iraqi lives, when he took office.

His plans to end the conflict, though, have been undone by Iraq's poisonous sectarian politics, Iranian meddling, his own mistakes and the devastating civil war across the border in Syria.

But they could not do the job of diplomats and civilian advisers who would stay behind after the troops came home to help the Iraqis forge a lasting peace.

"We'll help Iraqis strengthen institutions that are just, representative and accountable," Obama promised. "We'll build new ties of trade and of commerce, culture and education that unleash the potential of the Iraqi people."

But the final hours of the American occupation suggested a very different end.

We expect our wars to end in iconic moments.

"It's harder to end a war than begin one,"

The American military's top brass gathered at Baghdad International Airport to mark what was supposed to be the end of the war. Defense Secretary Leon E. Panetta offered up the usual praise for the troops. Gen. Lloyd Austin, who had pressed to keep a force of as many as 15,000 American troops in the country, gave a half-hearted endorsement to the proceedings, pronouncing Iraq a "relatively peaceful environment."

The Iraqis offered up the ceremony's most powerful statement by refusing at the last minute to attend.

Why does the United States struggle in war? How can it resolve a failing conflict? Can America return to victory?

Today, these are critical questions because we live in an age of unwinnable conflicts, where decisive triumph has proved to be a pipe dream. Indeed, power is part of the reason the United States loses. Nuclear deterrence stabilized relations between major states. The spread of democracy cultivated a zone of peace among elected regimes. Globalization and international trade deepened the linkages between countries and made interstate conflict seem costly or irrational.

But now the bad news: Conflict still exists in the form of civil wars or organized violence within the boundaries of a state. Nuclear weapons, democracy, and trade may stop countries from invading each other, but they don't prevent guerrillas, today about 90 percent of conflicts are civil wars. Global warfare is mainly relegated to a few dozen failed or failing states that are breeding grounds for warlords, insurgents, and criminals.

The shift from conflicts *between* countries to conflicts *within* countries triggered an era of American military failure. The United States waded into far-flung quarrels featuring culturally alien enemies, including North Korean, Chinese, and Vietnamese communists, Afghan insurgents, and Iraqi guerrillas handing the opponent home-field advantage.

The Iraq War has technically been over for more than four years, but Iraqis are still dying in large numbers. According to a U.N. report released Tuesday, nearly 19,000 Iraqis died between January 2014 and October 2015 due to continued instability in the country.

If one could push a button and end war on planet Earth, would you do it? How would a global farewell to arms change the planet, and how would we handle the realized dream of world peace.

War as a state of armed conflict between states or nations; you push that magic button and war as we've defined it ceases to be a possibility.

Let's have a great beginning to embrace peace with heartening support on both sides of the aisle.

If you could push a button and end war on planet Earth, would you do it? How would a global farewell to arms change the planet, and how would we handle the realized dream of world peace?

For starters, we have to decide exactly what we mean by "war."
Philosophers and politicians have spent thousands of years
wrestling with the term, but warfare dogs create situations of

war; they don't begin it, below their cunning innocence, there is a heap of well strategic alignment of war, the most authencity in the facts, but who may verify the facts. In war afflicted areas, children and women are easily be caught by rage of extremism; women are raped and children are killed without any tinge of mercy.

Awake while peace lying dead nearby
Silent nevertheless guns were fired
Hauled ma frame as a slave
Ma land got thy hands on
I got a whiff of blood
Sight of my broken toys and torn books
Mother's kitchen garden trodden down
Daddy...are you there
Aye ! knew he perished as a dead bird
Now I turned as a slave to my enemy
thee fed me well
kept me as clipped my feathers
all in all squeezed my liberty

Thou self-confessed as ma master
mine bows to thine notorious
world erected a statue to the most generous benefactor
the lords compelled me to hand over the harvest
by loving my enemy nearby

My endeavors under the barren tree
My feet walked over an isle of death
Treaded over yellow crumpled leaves
Wore scarlet drape
Meditated in magnificent frequency
Bird's chirp hallucinate my faculty
Whereof far is the piece of peace

Hauled frame as a slave

Ma land got thy hands on

I got a whiff of blood

Sight of my broken toys and torn books

Lost impoverished life

Nevertheless emotive accounts tangential

War is an oppressive tradition

Seeped in values of life

Death weaving through war inflicted narrow streets

Ugliness fueled by war

9 781981 235001